# World in a Shoe

## *My Journey with Horses*

Nicole Lawrence

# World in a Shoe
*My Journey With Horses*

© 2015 Nicole Lawrence

First Edition
All Rights Reserved. The author grants no assignable permission to reproduce for resale or redistribution. This license is limited to the individual purchaser and does not extend to others. Permission to reproduce these materials for any other purpose must be obtained in writing from the publisher except for the use of brief quotations within book chapters.

**Disclaimer**
Recognizing that, like most people, I don't have a perfect memory, I've recalled events to the best of my ability. Whenever possible, I contacted people integral to my experience for permission to use their real names. In instances where there was no way to reach someone for permission, those names were changed. In cases of a passing mention of someone not integral to the narrative, I left their real name and/or nickname.

The author of this book does not advise or prescribe any particular training methods, techniques or healing treatments for people to use with their horses. The intent of the author is only to convey her own experiences. In the event you use any of the information in this book for yourself, which is your Constitutional right, the author and the publisher assume no responsibility for your actions.

**Also by Nicole Lawrence**
"Doors to Transformation: My Mother – My Self"
For more information or to contact Nicole, go to http://nicolelawrence.com

**Front cover design:** Nicole Lawrence
**Back cover author portrait:** Carrie Mackey Photography

ISBN 10: 1-942731-16-7
ISBN 13: 978-1-942731-16-0

Published by M&B Global Solutions Inc.
United States of America (USA)

# Dedication

*For Robbyn P. and Michael C. - This is part of the song my
Soul wanted to sing.*

*To the horse trainer, John S. Heffner, his wife, Dottie, and their children,
Charlotte, Johnny, Michael and Rachel.
Thank You - I never did stop at the club on my way home.*

# Contents

Preface ............................................................................................ 9
Chapter 1 – Just Put Your Hand Out .......................................... 11
Chapter 2 – My Love of Horses Was Destined ......................... 15
Chapter 3 – We're Really Not Wanted ....................................... 19
Chapter 4 – Horses Were My Solace ........................................... 23
Chapter 5 – A Horse's Hoof Print ............................................... 27
Chapter 6 – Carried Along in the Wave ..................................... 31
Chapter 7 – The Darkness in the Barn ....................................... 35
Chapter 8 – Doors to Deeper Learning ...................................... 43
Chapter 9 – A Bunch of Amateurs .............................................. 47
Chapter 10 – Your Hand On That Stall Door ........................... 53
Chapter 11 – Take a Walk, Kid .................................................... 57
Chapter 12 – Talk is Cheap ........................................................... 61
Chapter 13 – It Doesn't Take Six Years ...................................... 67
Chapter 14 – The Chestnut Pony ................................................ 71
Chapter 15 - The Kokomo Kid .................................................... 75
Chapter 16 – I Knew It Was Horses for Me .............................. 81
Chapter 17 – Morven Park ........................................................... 83
Chapter 18 – Explain ..................................................................... 87
Chapter 19 – Porlock Vale in England ....................................... 91

# Contents

Chapter 20 – More Frightened Than Aggressive ...................... 95
Chapter 21 – She Really Did Want to Canter............................ 101
Chapter 22 – Lee ......................................................................... 107
Chapter 23 – Cahoon Nights...................................................... 115
Chapter 24 – Philbee................................................................... 121
Chapter 25 – Jokes and Vacation .............................................. 129
Chapter 26 – John Randall......................................................... 131
Chapter 27 – New Faces ............................................................. 135
Chapter 28 – Nahma................................................................... 139
Chapter 29 – Waves of Instinctive Action................................ 143
Chapter 30 – Delaware Park ...................................................... 147
Chapter 31 – Just Business ........................................................ 155
Chapter 32 – Any Vet to the Track ........................................... 161
Chapter 33 – Rodeo Cowboy ..................................................... 167
Chapter 34 – My Door's Always Open to You ........................ 171
Chapter 35 – World in a Shoe ................................................... 175
Epilogue........................................................................................ 177
Acknowledgements .................................................................... 179
About the Author........................................................................ 181

*World in a Shoe*

# Preface

A five-inch world framed within a horse's shoe. It hung on our dining room wall when I was growing up. To me, it was an icon of near mystical and religious significance. It riveted my adolescent fascination. I held it often, hoping to divine something out of its depths.

Clasped within its steel arms was a grainy, black-and-white photo of a horse standing in a winner's circle with a jockey astride. Unnamed men and women in coats and hats posed behind them. White, script lettering across the top spelled out "Rose Trellis."

Mom only ever said it was a gift; and that Rose Trellis, the horse in the photo, had worn the shoe when it won the race.

I thought about the shoe, its journey through time and across miles. Pressed into intimacy with mud, rocks, grit and grassy turf, the geography of terrain was its memoir. During its life, it cushioned the horse's prancing steps, settled firmly in the gentle dirt of doggedly boring walks around the shed row, and unerringly supported the relentless drive of competition. In retirement, it preserved a memory of success.

Entranced, I'd move my fingers over the worn and abraded places on the cool metal. My mind filled with images: horses bunched, running on the turn, muscles straining; thundering hooves pounding through sand; a flashing glint of metallic shoe crossing the finish line in victory.

\* \* \* \* \*

My passion for horses didn't arrive in my teenage years, as it does for many girls. It was deep and abiding for as long as I can remember. I set my sights on horses as my career from a very young age. I wasn't old enough to know the various disciplines in the horse world. I just knew I had to be with them. For me, it was like breathing.

My family thought I'd grow out of it. I didn't. They told me I'd grow up and get married, have kids; that my love of horses would fade. I didn't get married or have kids, but eventually I was separated from my life and love of horses for reasons my Soul, Spirit and the Divine knew, and I had to journey to find out.

As a child and adolescent, I ate, slept and dreamt horses. My passion afforded me many learning experiences, and at times, horses were a refuge and source of healing in my troubled life.

This book is my journey of my time with horses. As with Rose Trellis' shoe - called a racing plate in the business - this memoir covers many emotional terrains. Idealistic fantasies gained from reading fictional horse stories gave way, sometimes with brutal honesty, to the realities that can be found in the horse world. Along the way, I was helped by my mentor, who filled in as a father figure and gave me the guidance my alcoholic mother could not. In all, it was a tremendous learning experience. Horses themselves are some of the best teachers.

## Chapter 1

# Just Put Your Hand Out

From the time I figured out that being asked what I wanted for Christmas had anything to do with what showed up under the tree, I started begging for a horse.

Most years, I got something I was hoping for from my list amid snowflake yoke sweaters, scarves and underwear. Often I received toy horses, wonderful plastic models in many poses: standing, rearing and jumping. All of them stretched my imagination and I'd lose myself for hours playing with them.

I'd pretend they were in horse shows. Crawling on my hands and knees, I took the small statues on trail rides, "galloping" them along the carpet inside, and in the grass and under the rhododendrons outside. I'd stand books on end to make stalls, or cut up cardboard boxes to make stables the way I'd seen my sister, Debbie, do.

When I tired of that, I imagined being a horse myself. I would lay the benches from the picnic table on their sides in the yard, and then canter around, jumping the course of fences.

One Christmas, I was given a set of cartoon books titled "Thellwell Ponies." I remember one drawing in particular of a young girl running after the family dog, holding a small saddle in front of her. The caption read, "How to know when your child is ready for a pony." That was me.

My tenth Christmas arrived and again I asked for a horse - my standard first choice, followed by a bike and assorted other things. Each time I asked, I hoped to get something closer to a live horse, but I knew it was a lost cause. We lived in the suburbs, the houses on manicured lawns a stone's throw from each other. We did not have enough land for a pasture, let alone a barn. By process of elimination, as I explained to a friend on the phone Christmas Eve, I decided I was getting a new bicycle.

Christmas morning arrived and I dug through my stocking. It was my mother's habit to leave it outside my door to find in the morning. It was hard to be patient. The small presents – a chocolate apple and an orange tucked in the toe – were meant to entertain me until she woke up. I wasn't supposed to go downstairs or near the tree until she'd had her breakfast of black coffee and tomato juice.

Some holidays, Mom invited friends over in the morning for opening presents and then I had to wait until they arrived. This year, though, it was just the two of us. The others were coming later in the day and staying for dinner.

When it was finally time, I made a beeline for the tree. Mom followed with a second cup of coffee. I got a little toy barn that folded up like a suitcase with a latch. It had stalls and came with two plastic horses and a foal. I had opened my other presents and was playing with the miniature horse and stable set when Mom said, "Well, there's another present for you, but I wasn't able to get it delivered 'til around noon today."

Mom was up to her tricks again. Last year she had surprised me with a puppy. She got our next-door neighbor's son to bring it back from the kennel Christmas Eve in a driving snowstorm. My mother loved arranging surprises for people, and orchestrated the giving and often the receiving, too. For her, everything had to be just right and she staged all the details. Mom called the Mark family, our next-door neighbors and her partners in surprise crime, and arranged for me to go to their house until this year's surprise was ready.

While it's been many years and my memory isn't perfect, I remember taking my new toy barn over to Mrs. Mark and having cookies and hot chocolate in her kitchen. I imagined pouring real oats, in a real pail, in a real stable. I didn't mind the wait. I could spend hours in my mind, exploring and being anyplace I chose.

The phone rang. Whatever the surprise was, it was now ready. Mr. and Mrs. Mark got me bundled up to go outside. Mr. Mark placed a plaid scarf over my eyes, explaining that Mom wanted me to wear a blindfold.

I remember thinking, "*This is pretty weird for a bicycle, but Mom really likes her surprises.*"

They guided me, one on each side, through the snowdrifts in the yard. "Step up over the snow bank. No, not there. Now step down." I wobbled along, keeping my balance with their hands on my arms.

I heard Mom excitedly say, "Oh. There she is!"

The hardness under my feet told me I was no longer in the Marks' front yard but was now on the street. They led me toward the sound of my mother's voice.

"Now, keep your eyes closed," Mom said as someone lifted the scarf from around my head.

"Honey, are you ready?" she asked. I nodded that I was.

"Just put your hand out..."

Satiny warmth filled my fingertips and my eyes flew open. A big, beautiful horse with a liquid brown gaze was calmly taking me in. Time stopped. I think I must have stopped breathing, too. I was lost in the vibrant being standing before me. *My own horse!*

The horse, Sungay, had on a new saddle and bridle. Carrie, the lady who gave up her Christmas morning to drive him to our house for my surprise, lifted me up onto his back. Everything looked different from up on Sungay. I could see the tops of people's heads. Carrie walked me up and down the street, and I didn't want to get off.

When I look back at the photos, my mother was hugging me and saying things, but I have no memory of what she said. For me, the horse was my only world. Many of our neighbors, alerted by Mom, had turned out with cameras and were waiting for me to be led out. Later, I reflected on how quiet everyone had been. Not a cough, sneeze or boot scuffle gave away their presence.

Mom arranged to keep the horse at a stable outside of the suburbs, where I took lessons to learn to ride and how to care for my horse. I could go there after school and on weekends.

That Christmas, I began a deeper acquaintance with the world of horses, something I'd only done previously in my imagination. It was a relationship that set the foundations for how I learned and perceived life, and it was a doorway through which some of the most important people came into my life.

## Chapter 2

# My Love of Horses Was Destined

Looking back, it seems my love of horses was destined. Many times while growing up, my mother told me the story of how, when she was pregnant with me, she liked to bet on racehorses. She had been keeping an eye on a horse named Nicole - the same name she had chosen for me. The horse had come close to winning, and each time it ran, the odds got a little higher. Mom was hoping for a prime return on a modest bet.

On a hot July day, Mom went into labor and was whisked off to the hospital. The horse was running that day and she was sure it would win this time. She told me she tried to convince the doctor to let her use the phone to place a bet.

"I was so angry with him. I just knew that horse was going to win that day and it was fabulous odds," she said. "He wouldn't even let me make a phone call."

It was a good day for those named Nicole. The horse came in first and I galloped into my life.

From as young as I can remember, I was drawn to horses. Life seemed to support my inclination, and the horse theme in one way or another kept showing up. The preschool I attended was in a remodeled stone barn. In one corner stood the remnants of a stall, plank walls with black iron bars above and all. It served as storage for the toys. I lay awake at naptime on the blue plastic mat, imagining a horse in there behind the walls.

For a time I went to a preschool with a large, sloping field that led to a fenced yard with a horse in it. Although we were forbidden to go that far across the field at recess, every chance I got I made it to the fence to watch the large brown horse. Sometimes the lady who owned him spoke with me and let me pet him. She showed me how to hold my hand out flat to give him the carrot she'd place in my palm.

Soon, one teacher or another would appear in the field and sternly point a finger. "Come away from there. You know you are not supposed to be this far away from the school! Didn't I tell you, young lady, you were not to go near the horse?" I didn't care.

After much foot stomping and demanding on the teacher's part, I'd turn away from the fence - the teacher's voice scolding me all the way back to the school. My mind was back with the horse and I was immune. They could berate me until they were blue in the face. I didn't care. I was always drawn to the horse.

In retrospect, I realize the teachers never came near the horse and fence. They stood in the field, hesitant to approach. I probably could have stayed near the horse all day, frustrating them until it was time for Mom to take me home.

Just about everyone on my father's side of the family had an interest in horses in some way. My parents divorced when I was around four, and while my brother and sister lived with my dad, I grew up with my mom in the suburbs with not a lot of exposure to actual live horses. Before we were separated, I remember my older sister, Debbie, reading me bedtime stories of horses and doing fun projects with horses.

It was only much later as a teenager that I understood my mother was an alcoholic and my sister was trying her best to take care of us.

My sister made wonderful toys out of the most ordinary objects. One time, she took a broomstick and got a white sock from somewhere. She stuffed the sock with cotton balls and tied it to the broomstick. Using a magic marker, she drew two ovals near the heel of the sock and two circles and a long line down near the toe. Mystified, I watched. She cut some yarn into short strips and glued them to the sock. Suddenly, I got it.

"It's a horse!" Debbie had made me a hobbyhorse.

My favorite bedtime story was "Misty of Chincoteague" by Marguerite Henry, with wonderful illustrations by Wesley Dennis. It is a story about a pony who lived on an island off the coast of Virginia. The wild ponies were rounded up and swum across a channel to a place called Chincoteague. In this story, some children adopted a pony and they all had adventures together. Debbie showed me the illustrations while reading to me, and I'd look and look at the brown and white pony.

My sister had a collection of plastic and china horses. I loved to look at these and sometimes, when we were all living together, she'd let me touch the small white ones but not the others.

Then my brother and sister went to live with my dad and there were no more bedtime readings of "Misty of Chincoteague." One night, my dad came to the house with Debbie. He had an argument with Mom and left with all of Debbie's toys, including the horses.

I was distraught. The suddenness of them arriving, the arguing and the vehemence of my dad were enough to get me crying. I remember I wanted one of the horses, perhaps as a reminder of my sister, some form of connection to her. Mom begged him to leave just one for me. Dad was having none of it.

The next day my mother bought me a plastic horse, a Breyer model, an Appaloosa - white with little black spots all over. It had one front hoof raised and a little chain for reins. I think I named him Robby.

That first day I played on the floor for hours, running Robby around the patterns on the Oriental rug in Mom's room. Other toy horses followed with some pleading on my part, and Breyer models became standard presents for birthdays and Christmas.

But toys could not take the place of real, live horses. And real, live horses and ponies were what my grandmother had at her farm.

*World in a Shoe*

*Chapter 3*

# We're Not Really Wanted

My mother had married into and divorced out of a well-known family in the area. My father's family had a long history with horses and was – or had been – involved in almost every variety of horse sports you could think of. My grandparents had racehorses, foxhunters, steeplechasers, show horses and ponies. My father, aunts and uncles learned to ride as children. It was part of their lifestyle. Most stayed involved with horses in one way or another – breeding, sporting events or just riding for pleasure.

Whenever we went to visit relatives who had horses, the first thing I wanted to do was go to the barns. I'd squirm and wait impatiently while the grownups talked about non-horse, grownup stuff. My heart and mind were down in the stables, places of wonder to me.

If I got to the barns - always supervised - I'd peer in each stall looking for the gentle giants. An empty stall brought a wave of disappointment. But I knew where to look. If the horses weren't in the barns, they'd be out in the paddocks eating grass.

The adults always told me not to climb through the fence. So I'd stand at the railing, longing for the horses to come over. Generally, though, they had their minds on grazing.

Granny, my father's mother and the matriarch of the family, lived on a large estate about an hour's drive from us and had horses and ponies. She had horses for foxhunting, but was known for the Welsh ponies she bred, raised and showed.

An avid horsewoman, she was born and raised in an era when "polite" ladies did not ride astride, but sidesaddle. She continued to "ride to hounds," or fox hunt, sidesaddle into her eighties. Granny used the Welsh ponies she raised for driving carriages for pleasure and to compete. She drove everything from singles (one pony), pairs (two side by side), and tandems (one in front of the other) to a four-in-hand (four ponies pulling the carriage).

Granny explained to me that before the age of horse vans, driving two horses tandem was the mode of transportation to get to fox hunting meets. At times, one had to travel miles to where the hounds and riders were congregating. The horse in back, hooked to the carriage, did the work of pulling, while the front horse, the one to be ridden in the foxhunt, arrived fresh and ready.

My grandmother's farm was like a wonderland to me. We didn't go that often and even less after the divorce. Mostly, visits to my grandmother consisted of a swim in her pool or going to a party she hosted. Swimming afforded the most tantalizing option of seeing the horses and ponies, as the pool was nearer the barns than Granny's house. When our family was still together, Mom sometimes allowed Debbie to take Larry and me to the first couple of barns to look at them. I knew the names of the different buildings painted white with green trim: hunter barn, pony barn, racehorse barn, among others. The barns were always peaceful and quiet. The shady coolness within was soothing compared to the hot summer sun outside. The horses usually were outside in the fields, but sometimes we'd be rewarded with an inquisitive nose poked in our direction. I would have loved the freedom to run all over, but I wasn't allowed to go exploring on my own.

I had my very first ride on the back of one of my grandmother's ponies. I must have been four or so. Mom and I were visiting and she took us down to one of the pony barns. One of the men who worked for her got out a beautiful white pony named Susie. The man lifted me up onto the pony's round back and Granny took the lead line. Telling me to hold on tight, she walked me around a small paddock. I didn't want to get off, and only Mom's insistence that it was time to go made me release Susie's fluffy white mane.

I loved the smell of horse on my fingers after being entwined in Susie's long hair. If I could keep that smell, I could conjure the image and feeling of the warm body and smooth coat beneath my fingers, feel the soft whiskers and velvety nose, see the color of the big, liquid brown eyes, and feel the rise of her back when she took a breath. In my imagination, I could still feel the coarse mane wrapped around my fingers.

After the divorce, Mom and I didn't go to see Granny that often. If it was to swim, Mom always took us to the house to thank Granny afterwards. Oil paintings of the horses Granny had owned hung on the walls of the front hall. We sat in overstuffed, flower-print chairs beside delicate side tables that held small vases of fresh-cut flowers or orchids.

I remember a lot of silences and not much conversation. Granny always asked if we had a good swim and I always asked if I could pet the ponies. Usually she replied, "No, Dearie, not today. Maybe another time you can pet the ponies."

Granny was always nice to me, though I never felt the kind of closeness that would have made it possible for me to climb into her lap. There was a distance whenever I was around her; a reserve, a sense that some things were "proper" and others not. Secretly, I wanted her to show me the ponies, teach me to ride and tell me stories about all of her horses. Instead, I sensed there was an unspoken standard expected of me; one that I met less and less over the years. The closest I ever got to stories was when she visited me in the hospital after a car accident. She got me to eat something I hated (Lime Jell-O) by having me take a bite for each of her ponies.

I never understood why Granny, the one with horses, gave me those wool, snowflake yoke patterned sweaters every Christmas. I thought surely she would give me something with a horse on it, but it was always one of those sweaters in a different color.

I'd heard about the overnights that Debbie, who was eight years older than me, got to go on: weekends at Granny's. My brother, Larry, also got a chance to stay at Granny's. They went without Mom or Dad and got to stay for the whole weekend. I begged to go also and was always told, "When you are older."

Even though I was five when I went to live alone with Mom, I dreamed of the time I'd get to go to Granny's. I wanted to ride ponies and have Granny tell me about horses all day long.

As my sixth birthday approached, I held the hope of staying at Granny's. Maybe at six I'd be old enough to go. I don't remember the exact conversation, but Mom made it clear I wasn't welcome at Granny's.

"Can I go stay at Granny's?" I asked.

"No, you can't go." Mom replied.

I reminded her that she told me I could go when I was old enough. This time it wasn't about being old enough.

"Oh, honey, things have changed. Granny is your Dad's mom. Now that he and I are divorced, it's like we are the black sheep of the family. We're not really wanted there."

I was upset and despondent, my little hopes dashed. Somehow that opportunity had passed me by due to the actions of the grownups around me. I had no control over any of it.

Solace lay with my toy horses, which is where I went after talking to Mom. Cantering the plastic models around on the rug in my room, I imagined the living, breathing, real-life thing. I determined that somehow, one way or another, I was going to have a life involving horses.

Less and less did I get to go to Granny's outside of the few, annual parties she invited my mom to attend. Our visits were brief amid crowds of people, and when I wanted to swim in the summers, Mom instead took me to a local college pool where she had taken out a membership.

## Chapter 4

# Horses Were My Solace

What I didn't understand as a child was that my mother was an alcoholic. Nights alone with her were traumatic because of her drinking, and I now suspect she took pills as well.

Stability had come from my sister. But without Debbie to look after me, I was no longer shielded from my mother's crazy behavior. There was no dinner on the many nights my mother was passed out. No one to tuck me into bed or read a bedtime story. Sometimes she hallucinated people that weren't there. I think my mom's parents thought my dad was looking out for me, and he thought my mother's parents were doing the same.

I was alone a lot and felt the separation from Debbie and Larry. For the most part, I figured out how to fend for myself. I spent a lot of time in my imagination, playing with my toy horses.

Horses, in one form or another, were my solace, even in my dreams. I had a recurring one that came after some of the hardest times with my mother.

I was up high on a catwalk or balcony. Below me, nestled in golden-yellow straw, were white Pegasus horses. A woman in a long gown was talking to me while I looked at their snowy backs and curved wings.

Whenever I woke from this dream, I was filled with a sense of peace and wholeness. My little body vibrated with a deep peace and feeling of safety. I loved having this dream. I was always renewed afterward. Life didn't seem so hard and whatever fears I'd experienced were washed away. The deep, centered stillness stayed with me, sometimes for days. I consider this dream as one of the things that helped me get through my childhood.

\* \* \* \*

Though I couldn't have the weekend visits with Granny, I could still get to see live horses. One of my happier memories is of Mom taking me to the Devon Horse Show and Country Fair in Devon, Pennsylvania. We'd go at least one of the days the show was on. I'm sure I begged for more - I could have gone every day and not had my fill.

Every year at the end of May, champion horses and riders arrive from all over the country to participate in ten days of competition. It is a big annual event. Even those not involved with horses go for the fair and midway.

Devon is unique in that various disciplines in the world of horse sports are represented. Equines of all shapes and sizes, from small ponies to giant carriage horses, can be seen. I could have watched the horses all day, but Mom liked to see the shops at the country fair.

The shops were little, playhouse-sized buildings grouped together as a kind of village. Painted white with light blue trim, the shops were adorned by red geraniums in the miniature flower boxes below the windows.

Local vendors rented these shops to sell their wares: clothing, shoes, handbags, wrap-around skirts, scarves, kitchen cutlery, needlepoint and knickknacks – all with an equine theme. Other shops sold food items: jams and jellies, crackers, cookies and the famous Devon fudge. Teenage girls walked the grounds carrying basket-trays selling fresh lemons with a candy stick in them.

To me, the best shops sold horse equipment. Called tack shops, they contained bridles, saddles and all manner of horse equipment. I eagerly stepped into these tiny spaces crowded with pungent leather goods. The new, light tan, untreated leather was waxy under my fingertips. I remember being impatient with Mom. She wanted to visit all the clothing shops and barely gave me time to look in the tack shops.

The midway was games, rides, calliope-like music and kids running and screaming. The best thing about the midway was the pony rides, and I could always get Mom to get me a ride.

Beyond the midway lay the barns - my favorite part of the show grounds. I loved to go in them, anything to bring me closer to what was happening with the horses.

The stables were a hive of activity. Horses crossed and crisscrossed in all directions. Children walked ahead of ponies and grooms led carriage horses in full harness with large collars, their hooves scrunching on the gravel, metal shoes making tinny sounds on the rocks.

Grooms and riders engaged in activities to prepare their horses for the show ring: brushing, braiding and cleaning tack. A groom scrubbed and rinsed a horse's legs. Another horse, just bathed, swished his tail and an arc of water flew by.

All about me I heard the clanking of metal and creaking of leather as the horses in their many sizes and colors passed on their way to the show ring or back to their barns.

I hated having to leave the show. Mom usually bought me a souvenir. One year it was a key chain with clear plastic fob of the Devon logo; another it was a little china horse with rabbit's fur main and tail. Every year, she bought a show program. It was the size of a small-town phone book and contained the names of all the exhibitors, classes, advertising from local businesses, and photographs of horses and riders of years gone by. I'd savor that book for a long time - the pictures inspiring fantasies and dreams.

Mom knew I loved horses. Why they meant so much to me, I don't think she could understand. I'm not even sure I understood. I just knew they were magical beings.

*World in a Shoe*

## Chapter 5

# A Horse's Hoof Print

When the Devon show ended, I felt lost for my next horse fix. I knew horses lived in pastures, and for me, behind every fence in the neighborhood lay the possibility of a horse. In the typical suburban area we lived in, people used fences as decorations and to define the limits of their property. Sometimes, though, they'd have a backyard horse. Whenever we drove by a fence, I'd search the grassy yard beyond for a sleek, shiny-coated horse. I was disappointed when the fence was purely decorative. What good was having a fence if you couldn't put a horse behind it?

When I was in fourth grade, my mother moved us to a new neighborhood. It was typical upper middle-class. Each house had its square of lawn with old trees spreading shade, with cul-de-sacs and winding lanes leading to corner school bus stops. I knew we didn't have any horses in my immediate neighborhood - I'd ridden my bike through every road, lane and cul-de-sac in search of one. But this neighborhood did hold a secret. Hidden away behind backyard fences and the grassy stop of dead-end lanes was a place forgotten by the rest of the world.

I discovered it by chance, wandering down a "no outlet" street. Where the road dead-ended at a wall of forest, I noticed an overgrown passage curving away into the woods under the canopy of trees and bushes. What was once a gravel drive for cars was now pot-holed, covered with weeds and the litter of fallen limbs and branches.

It was way too much of a draw for a nine-year-old to resist. I made my way among the weeds and saplings. At a curve in the drive, the forest parted, opening onto a field barred by a large wooden gate - the type you see on farms. Ever hopeful, I approached with one thought: "Horses?"

I was disappointed to see the gate was freestanding and not connected to a fence on either side. It seemed the field was not meant to contain anything like a horse, and the gate was just to deter entry. Even though the gate had a heavy chain and padlock on it, I had no trouble slipping between the post and green vines to step out into the overgrown meadow. *"This would be a great place to keep a horse,"* I thought to myself. But I could see the space was already somebody's front yard – or what was left of it. Up the gentle slope, I could make out the burned foundations of what had once been a mansion.

Cautiously, I wandered a little way out into the field populated by wildflowers and tall grasses. I stood and looked around. *"What is this place?"* I wondered.

I don't remember whom I asked, but I later learned it was called the old Schmidt estate. No one seemed to know who the Schmidts were and no one had lived there for a very long time. It seemed to have once been a grand place, yet for whatever reason had been abandoned years before we moved to that neighborhood and remained so until we moved away nearly ten years later.

Realizing there was no one to chase me away, I returned again and again on weekends and sometimes after school to explore. Mostly I made my excursions into the estate alone or with our dogs. I don't remember the other children of the neighborhood going in there. They must have found it as irresistible as I did, yet I never saw anyone else there.

The estate grounds were a place of mystery and adventure. It was a place of more questions than answers. Throughout the grounds were a gazebo, broken statues covered in vines, a few smaller sheds and what could have been a cow barn. The main house was nothing but a burnt hole in the ground. One or two blackened beams suggested there had been a fire. What had happened?

Anything that had been a tended garden or lawn was long overgrown with weeds and meadow grasses. Since the estate was large, I just knew there had to have been horses there as well, but I could find no horse barns on the grounds.

Beyond the old farm buildings was a small, iron-fenced enclosure choked with waist-high weeds, thistles and vines. In the center of this tangle stood a neglected wisteria arbor. Great cement pillars, two feet across, rose in pairs from the underbrush, with wisteria and ivies hanging from the iron rebar across the top.

One lazy summer afternoon, with nothing to do, I ventured into the sun-dappled shade of the estate. I topped the hill out of the meadow and passed by the weathered outbuildings. It was the middle of the day; that still time when not much stirs other than a faint breeze swaying the tops of the grassy seed heads. Silence is the loudest sound, broken occasionally by a few grasshoppers singing, cicadas thrumming, bees mildly buzzing, and somewhere, a robin chirping in a tree. The sun was hot, and I followed a gentle breeze as it meandered toward the wisteria arbor.

Vines nearly covered the columns, the pale purple flowers of wisteria peeking through in clumps. The smell was heavy and pungent, almost a sting in my nose. I usually just explored outside of the iron fence; going into the arbor itself was almost impossible because of the matted thicket of vines, shrubs and poison ivy growing beneath.

Today I decided to venture in. I climbed the fence, and as I swung my leg over the top, I looked down and stopped. Preserved in the dried dirt – as though cast in plaster – was a horse's hoof print.

My heart skipped a beat. There were horses in here somewhere. Gently, I let myself down into the high field grasses and Queen Anne's lace. I had been in the estate many times and had never seen any sign of horses. Scanning as far as I could see around the shrubs and trees, I made my way across the field. My instincts were good and I spotted not one, but two horses foraging in the grass. As I approached, they lifted their heads; a gray and a bay with a halter on.

They had to belong to someone. I had to find out whom.

I clamored out of the field and trotted down the overgrown lane to where the county blacktop began. I went to the first house I saw - a large, three-story, ivy-covered stone house with green shade awnings on the windows. I rang the bell and a kindly, elderly lady answered. Yes, the horses belonged to her daughter. Yes, I could come back when her daughter was there. And yes, I could probably have a ride on one of the horses supervised by her daughter; but please don't go into the field alone with the horses.

Her daughter was leaving for college in a few weeks and the horses were being moved to a new stable. They were only there for a short time. Since no one lived at the old Schmidt estate anymore, they didn't think anyone would mind if they kept the horses in the field temporarily. Who was to know? Who was around to ask?

I did get my ride and I visited the horses often that summer. Then one afternoon, they were gone. No one answered at the house.

September had arrived and it was also time for me to be back in school. I returned to the arbor often that fall and relived my memories of those horses. The hoof prints by the fence stayed there until the winter rains washed them away.

## Chapter 6

# Carried Along in the Wave

In spite of my family's background with horses and my grandmother's distance, I finally had my very own horse. He was stabled at a farm in the Malvern area, not far from Philadelphia – definitely horse country. Although I'd had riding lessons in the past, I learned a great deal more. Now I was also learning how to care for him.

It was a whole new world. I learned how to muck stalls and clean my saddle and bridle, called "tack" in the horse world. I examined handfuls of sweet feed – a mixture of oats, corn, molasses and other things that are food for horses. I even tried to eat some. The oats and corn were too hard to chew, but I sucked on the kernels to get the sweet molasses off. It was slightly salty, but not nearly as salty as the bricks called "Salt Licks" that were in the stalls and pastures for the horses.

I watched the farrier trim the horse's hooves, and then shape and fit the metal shoe before nailing it on. When the blacksmith held the hot shoe in place, the smoke and sizzle of the horse's hoof smelled like burned hair in a candle flame. I was a pest and asked all kinds of questions about whether or not the horse could feel it and why it didn't hurt to put nails in his feet. The farrier was very patient. He explained a horse's hoof has an outer layer like our fingernails that doesn't have feeling. As long as the nails are in the right place, it doesn't hurt the horse.

The riding stable was an old farm with a barn and many outbuildings that had also been converted to house horses. I spent every day I could there.

It was important that I have lessons not only on my own horse, but on some of the other lesson horses as well. Experience with different horses improves you as a rider. Lots of children rode at the farm where my horse was stabled, and on weekends there were packs of us running around. The owners of the farm taught the lessons, and we helped with the grooming, tacking up, filling water buckets and all the things that go on anywhere kids and horses come together.

The lesson horses didn't have their own stalls. They lived in the pasture behind the barn. The stalls were for boarders - people who paid to have their horses live inside, and turned out or ridden during the day.

The horses that lived outside needed to be caught for the lessons. That usually required a trek through the field, picking a path across a meandering creak and hiking up a long hill. During the heat of the day, the horses would retreat to the shade of the trees at the crest of the hill.

Often, only two or three horses were needed for lessons. It was a lot of walking back and forth. One day, one of the older kids tossed me a loop of baling twine from a bale of hay. I asked about bringing halters and lead ropes, but she said no, just come on, and we headed out into the field.

Reaching the horses, we found the ones we wanted. I watched her slip the twine into its mouth, making a loop around the horse's neck to serve as the reins, like an Indian pony. Grabbing a handful of mane, she leapt up onto the horse's back. I followed her lead with the twine and struggled onto the horse I was bringing in.

We rode them bareback, at a walk, down the hill and across the pasture. I could feel the horse's back and shoulder muscles bunching and flowing beneath my legs as he strode through the tall grass, his back swaying rhythmically. Sliding off at the gate, I had short brown hairs all along the inside of my jeans. The hairs began itching as they worked their way through the fabric.

I don't think we were supposed to ride the horses in, but the hill was out of sight of the main farm buildings and no one ever seemed to see us. It was less walking and a lot more fun, I thought, until one day I went out alone to get a pinto horse.

We started lazily back down the field when I heard rumbling thunder behind me. The little horse picked up his head, tensed his back and swiveled his ears to catch every sound. The other twenty or so horses in the field decided to run to the barn. In two strides, the pinto matched his friends and I found myself surrounded by black, brown and gray galloping backs, manes streaming in the wind. I discovered the baling twine was next to useless for any sort of stopping or turning. All I could do was grab the mane and hang on.

Being part of a band of horses running flat-out was exhilarating, while at the same time I had snatches of the realization that, if I fell off, I'd be under many pounding hooves. As a herd, we swept down the hill, leapt the stream and ran up the rise to the barn.

I was carried along in the wave to a sliding stop in the throng of horses at the gate. Hopping off – a little shaken, but none the worse for wear – I decided it would be safer in the future to lead horses in on foot, with a halter and rope, than to be careening downhill, bareback, without head protection and little or no control.

One morning, I walked out to get a lesson horse. I noticed a chestnut mare, barely able to stand, her head hanging to the ground. I knew something was wrong and I ran to get help. She was all beaten up, big bite marks and strips of skin missing. One eye was swollen shut, her head cut and lacerated.

I had never seen a horse so injured. Along the fence line, the grass and dirt was torn up. The owners determined the fence had been struck by lightning from the storm the night before and the mare standing near it had gotten a secondary strike. Then the other horses in the field had attacked her.

It was the first time I'd ever heard of this phenomenon, but it wasn't the last. Sometimes when an animal is injured, others of its own kind will turn on it and try to kill it. Years later I heard of another instance, and witnessed it myself at a livestock sale where horses were kept in pens together.

The mare from the field was given a stall in the barn. The owners told us they were going to try and nurse her back to health. But one day she was gone. When I asked about her, they said she wasn't getting better. In fact, the horse had never been right after being struck by the lightening that night. They had to sell her.

*Chapter 7*

# The Darkness in the Barn

I don't remember how I met Jill. I think her mom was a friend of my mom's. Her parents were divorced, and she and her younger brother lived with her mom, like I did mine. Her mother must have indulged her because, though she was my age, she had three horses of varying sizes and temperaments.

I found her very difficult to be around. She had a strong personality and bossed everyone – even her mother – around. Her mother acquiesced to her every demand and put up with Jill criticizing and yelling at her. It was one of those passing friendships that only lasted for a year or so.

The Bicentennial occurred in 1976 during the time we were friends. As part of the celebrations, Conestoga Wagons and carts of all kinds traveled from across the country to Pennsylvania, pulled by horses, mules and oxen. Their purpose was to recreate, in reverse, the journey made by pioneers and settlers to the West. Seven routes led east and many of the wagon trains were on the road for more than a year. Their destination: Valley Forge Park. Jill's horses were stabled in a small barn near the park.

She invited me to go for a ride to see all the wagons, horses and people. It was early in the weeks-long celebration and some wagons had arrived, but not nearly the volume that eventually would fill the grassy fields of the park. We rode through the encampments, looking at the draft horses, the wagons from different states and all the people in period dress.

In particular, I remember a pair of yoked oxen that had pulled a covered wagon all the way from the Midwest. The oxen were placid, rust-colored giants with long, curving horns many feet across. It was like going back in time. Every effort was made to be authentic. People wandered around in period dress, carrying wooden platters piled with food. Even the water buckets were wooden slats with rope handles, and the animals were tethered in the old-fashioned way - on a picket line.

\* \* \* \*

For some reason, Jill never came to the farm where I had my horse. I didn't see her that often, with long periods of time between visits. Though I wasn't uncomfortable with that.

Riding different horses developed me as a rider. Each was unique. Some were eager to go while others poked along.

One little bay mare had a white star on her forehead that tapered into a marking – called a snip – over one nostril. It looked like someone had poured cream that flowed down her face and ran off the side of her nose, making half of it white.

She was feeling perky the day I rode her. When I gave the signal to canter, she tossed in a few bucks for free and off her back I went. Instinctively, I put my hands in front of me to break my fall. What I broke was my left wrist.

Having a cast and the manner in which I acquired it was considered somewhat exotic at school. My best friends drew pictures and wrote messages on the plaster. My only sorrow was that it kept me from riding for six weeks while it healed.

At least my broken arm happened in late spring, the time when the annual Devon Horse Show rolled around. Sometimes Mom dropped me off after school and I'd hang out at the show with friends or wander by myself. I looked forward to those afternoons, and on weekends it was pure bliss for me to spend whole days there.

I had a set pattern upon arrival. On the first afternoon, I'd go to the program stand to buy the book listing the show's competitors. Then I'd find a spot on the rail of the main ring to see what class was going on and peruse the program, looking to see if I recognized any names of horses and riders returning from previous years.

Once I'd looked over the program, I'd make a circuit of the tack shops to see what was new in horse equipment and then head in the direction of the stables. Even before I saw the farrier, I could hear the sound of hammering on the anvil in the long and short staccato rhythm peculiar to blacksmiths. Most shows provide the services of a farrier in case of a lost or loose shoe. Sometimes I stopped to watch him forge and shape the red-hot metal before putting it to sizzle in a bucket of water. I enjoyed all of the behind-the-scenes activities of the show, visiting barns and sometimes chatting with the grooms.

Because the show was ten days long, stabling was provided for the horses. Housing for the horses had grown over the years as the show's popularity increased. In those days, the older structures were painted pale blue with white trim, while the newer barns were a natural, stained wood.

Stalls are bedded down, aisles raked, bottles of liniment and tins of saddle soap unpacked, and buckets of soapy water and sponges appear in the wash areas. Grooms clean, polish and make last-minute adjustments to horses and tack. In the schooling and warm-up areas, riders move their mounts with focused determination to their next task. Throughout, the stables remain the quiet refuge in what looks like pandemonium to the uninitiated.

Approaching the barns, I saw horses being led back and forth, coats shining in the sunlight, manes and tails braided. Tacked up in polished leather, they were ready to compete in one of the two rings beside the grandstands. Grooms walked by with rub rags trailing from back pockets, carrying brushes and hoof picks.

I could name the tools and equipment used on horses, but back when I was little, with Mom ushering me around the show, all of the hustle and bustle seemed mysterious. Sometimes, with enough pleading, I could convince her to take me through the barns.

Now thirteen and on my own at the show grounds, I relished the freedom to do as I pleased. I could sit and watch the classes in the ring all day or hang around the barns as long as I wanted. Even the cast on my arm did not dim my excitement of watching the pre-competition preparations.

Stepping into the cool, horse-fragrant darkness was like crossing an invisible boundary to another world. Walking the dirt aisle way, carefully raked clean of bits of hay and straw, I strolled past stalls where animals rested when not needed in the ring.

The activity level was quieter inside the sanctuary of the barns. People moved in slower, more relaxed gestures. There was a kind of stillness, a hush where life became a gentle exhale.

Grooms, riders and trainers almost whispered as they went about their steady business. Listening to the sounds of the horses, I relaxed, feeling the tranquil rhythm of the barn.

I went back to the grandstand to find a seat on the bleachers and watch some afternoon classes.

"How'd you get that?"

I turned to the demanding voice behind me.

"Oh, hi Jill. I got tossed off riding."

"When?"

"A couple of weeks ago."

Her responding shrug could have meant "That's too bad," or it could have meant, "That's what happens to riders who aren't very good." I hadn't seen her in a long time, which was good because I could only take her acerbic nature in small doses. To her, if you weren't tough, you were a wuss.

Three or four other kids I didn't know came over to join us. No introductions.

"Go see what class is going on at the main ring," Jill commanded. Obedient acolytes, they went. "Students. I'm helping them with their riding," she explained before I could ask.

I was learning, and Jill already thought she knew it all.

I hung out with her at the show since I hadn't run into anyone else I knew. We walked around for a bit, and then watched a couple of classes.

We left the afternoon competition a little before it ended to get a bite to eat. I knew from experience that at the dinner break people would throng from the grandstands to wait in line for pizza, hot dogs, hamburgers, soft drinks and ice cream. As dusk increased, the lights came on in the main arena, signaling the activities were soon to begin. Shoppers poked around in the little gift booths on their way back to the grandstands for the evening performances.

Jill and I caught up with the other kids, whose names I still didn't know. Earlier in the day, they had spent some time talking to a groom from one of the stables who had come up from the south for the show. Going to the barns had more appeal for us than watching the classes in the ring. As a small band in the growing dark, we headed away from the crowds, noise and lights.

It felt important, hanging out - like we were part of things. It was just the groom, a man in his fifties, and us kids talking in the quiet barn. The other workers, trainers and riders were at the ring, watching the competition.

We asked him what it was like to work at the show, what kind of equipment he used and did his horses win a lot of ribbons. We were enthralled, and he seemed happy to entertain us.

Full night settled in beyond the open door. The only lights in the barn were where we sat asking questions and listening. The rest of the long building faded into an eerie blackness of shadowy forms.

Someone started kicking an empty soda can around, and soon we were all laughing and playing kick-the-can. I was cautious of my arm in its cast and stayed near the edge of the game to avoid being bumped. Even the groom joined in. Stocky and strong, dancing around, playing like he was one of us. Quick and agile, he mimicked our slang and laughed with us – but just a little out of sync, like he got the jokes a second too late. Something odd tugged at my mind, but I shook it off. I was having fun. One of the kids must have said something about getting soda or candy, because they all took off in a pack. One minute they were there, and the next I stood in an empty aisle.

Suddenly, dirty hands clamped over my mouth from behind. Locked in a vice grip, I froze. He dragged me into the darkness in the barn. The soda can in the dirt burned a snapshot in my vision. My mind stopped, perversely stuck on the thought, "Where did those kids go so fast?"

Dark hair askew, he breathed heavily with the effort of seizing onto me. I have no memory of how he got me down the aisle, into an empty stall where hay and straw bales were stacked.

"Go ahead and struggle," he grunted, pinning me against the hay bales. "It will only make it better." His sweaty face and grime-creased skin on his neck was inches from me. I no longer knew how to breathe. I had no voice. I only knew how to freeze.

"You're gonna love this," his gravelly voice hissed.

Yellowed teeth showed through a lopsided grin. "My dick's as hard as a rock. You can fight all you want, it's only gonna make it better."

Forcing me down with one arm, his other hand fumbled with his belt, pulling the leather out of the buckle.

I had no thoughts other than I wanted out. My mind shut off everything, narrowing down to a pinpoint of, "Let me go!" I wanted out, I wanted to get away. I couldn't speak, let alone yell. My voice was as frozen as the rest of my body. I saw his fingers reach to undo the button on his jeans.

Voices, outside. Approaching the side door of the barn.

"I don't know, I think we should let the poor horses get some sleep," a man said.

"Oh come on, I just want to have a look," a woman responded.

"Well, all right, but let's not take too long. It's getting late."

My attacker stopped. Before the people crossed the threshold, he spun and took off up the aisle.

Frozen in terror, I lay silent, watching from the shadows of the stall. They didn't see me as they passed by; two couples, the ladies talking and looking at the horses.

When they were gone, I ran the other way into the night.

Going straight to the gate to leave the fairgrounds, I saw Jill with the others. I pulled her aside, "That guy, he grabbed me. He..."

"He would never do that! That never happened!" she shouted. Turning, she angrily stalked away into the crowd.

I don't remember ever seeing or talking to Jill again after that night.

I never told my mother. She would have forbidden me to ever go back to the show. I didn't think I'd be allowed to go anywhere alone again. I would have lost any sense of freedom, and possibly even having horses in my life.

Had I spoken it, the fuss would have been huge given my family and its connections. I had already encountered so much looking and prying. I just couldn't stomach being the focus of any more intense scrutiny.

My mind didn't range around to think of all of the things that might have happened that night. I assumed, in part, that he'd grabbed me because my arm in a cast made me vulnerable. I was so naive that it was a couple of years before I even knew there was a word for what he'd tried to do to me.

I returned to the show the following year, but the magic of the barns was lost to me. For a long time, I could not wander them alone. I avoided the building where it happened because competitors often stabled in the same location year after year. I didn't want to chance ever seeing him again. When I did venture inside a barn, I'd wait until there was a group of people entering and surreptitiously slide in behind, as though I was with them. The stables were no longer places of quiet ease and safety for me. I was tense, cautious and watchful, hyperaware of each person at work and where they were in the barn.

I held my secret. From the deceptive view of a frightened mind, I talked myself into an unspoken pact, an agreement to not say anything. *"You got away, it was a near miss. It's not like anything actually happened."*

Yet in doing so, I wrote the fine print on my own contract of silence. I accepted the close call and my escape in exchange for never giving voice to what happened. It was a twisted kind of self-bargaining. For a long time I feared if I ever did tell, I would call into being something worse, something that would finish what had started. Time and life's experiences would prove the falsehood of the entire bargain.

*Chapter 8*

# Doors to Deeper Learning

Around this time, Mom decided to sell my horse to a family down the road from the farm. I was okay with it, since he was too big and strong for me and I had had some bad falls from him. He was a great horse, but simply too much for me. I wasn't riding him or going out to the farm all that often anymore.

One of my best friends in school was Missy. She was just as horse crazy as I was. Our sleepovers took place amidst eight-inch-high herds of plastic horses.

Although horseless, I still wanted to ride and take lessons. One day at school, a woman came to talk about starting a riding club. Of course, Missy and I had to be there. This was it. We had to go riding at that stable.

Thorncroft Equestrian Center was a full-on, teach-lessons-to-kids-all-day-long establishment. They had an indoor arena and held classes throughout the winter. There were some boarders, but the majority of their business was teaching. The barn was crawling with kids on the weekends.

It was a good place, and I had Missy to ride with. We became "barn bums" – teenagers who hang around at the barn helping out. We willingly mucked dirty stalls and carried heavy buckets of water, just happy to be there.

Every second of every weekend we could be at Thorncroft, we'd be there. We grew to know the lesson horses and all of their quirks. Missy liked a pale gray mare with dark gray markings called dapples

– which also happened to be the name of the horse. I liked Blackie, who was, of course, black.

We groaned or were delighted according to which horse we were assigned in our lessons. We didn't always get to ride our favorites. When it came to jumping, Space to Spare was the popular choice. We had to continually kick Make a Wish to keep him going with enough pep to clear the jumps. Spot, one of the Appaloosas, liked to stop and look at the fence. It took a lot of steering and leg to keep him going. Other horses, like fuzzy gray Malabar or jet-black Raven, you just pointed in the right direction and they did all the work themselves. When we became good enough, we competed in small schooling shows held in Thorncroft's indoor arena.

I went through a phase of intense nightmares in my teenage years. Airplane crashes, explosions and fires populated my nights. Some of them turned out to be premonition dreams – upsetting when I dreamed them, more so when they played out in real life.

The soothing Pegasus visions that visited my childhood dreams had long since faded into the past. Many mornings I'd jolt awake crying, thrown from the chaos of destruction back into my teenage life. I felt helpless to do anything in my disaster dreams.

One dream haunted me with its impact: a vivid nightmare of horses trapped in a barn while being burned in a fire. The next day I learned twenty-nine horses had died in a fire at Garden State Racetrack the night of the dream.

In my high school, some teachers showed short, Avant-guard films - some of them not even related to the subject being taught. My history and English teachers both showed the same films at different times throughout the year.

I only remember two of these films. One called "Hanging at Owl Creek Bridge" took place in the Civil War. The other, "A Dream of Wild Horses," was about a herd of horses in a watery wetland that get caught in a fire. I sat through it once. When it came around again in another classroom, I walked out, refusing to view it again. I was determined not to watch what I'd been seeing in my dreams.

In my senior year, I took an elective class on film and cinema. The teacher was planning to show "A Dream of Wild Horses." I told her I wouldn't watch it. She replied if I didn't she would fail me. Both of us stayed true to our word. None of the teachers ever asked why I wouldn't watch the film.

\* \* \* \*

It helped to be able to ride at Thorncroft. I continued to learn about caring for horses. There were a few instructors on staff, and we sometimes had lessons with different ones.

Some were easier on us than others, some more encouraging and others took us to task. They all pushed us past our current abilities - whether though balance exercises or building strength by posting the trot without stirrups - to keep improving as riders.

Three or four of the instructors had graduated from a professional riding school called Morven Park International Equestrian Institute. When we complained about how hard they were making us work, they'd tell us stories of what they'd gone through at Morven Park. What we were doing was nothing compared to their experiences.

They were professionals, and when we weren't riding they continued to teach us. I think it was Chris who brought a horse's leg to the barn. She wanted us to understand the mechanics of how the tendons and ligaments worked with each other. She had acquired the hind leg of a horse from a rendering plant and preserved it, keeping it in a garbage can with formaldehyde. She walked in the barn with this long, bent object wrapped in black plastic slung over her shoulder.

When she first unwrapped it, I felt like, *oh gross*. Then it was kind of cool. There was no skin or muscle, just the hoof, bones, ligaments and tendons. She showed us how the ligaments connect the joints together. The leg still had some flexibility, and when she pulled on a tendon, the hoof moved in response. I had never really thought much about what went on inside the horse's body before this. Later, I understood what an important lesson this was – especially in how an injury occurs and what happens in the healing process.

Missy and I continued to ride on weekends. But as sometimes happens with teenage friendships, we grew apart and she stopped riding at the stable.

I learned something about horses at each place I rode. At the stable where I had my first horse, I learned a lot of basics. Thorncroft hired certified and trained instructors who did more than teach us from the horse's back. I also had the opportunity to meet a more diverse group of horse professionals at Thorncroft that opened the doors to deeper learning.

## Chapter 9

# A Bunch of Amateurs

"Get away from that horse!" the man angrily yelled from the barn door. Startled, three people stopped their fight with the horse in the yard.

They were trying to load the animal onto a horse van – a large truck with a sloped ramp leading up to the compartment. Most horses are fine going up the incline into the covered van. Not all horses are easy about it, though, and some need encouragement. With a difficult horse, two or three people work together. Sometimes crossing ropes behind the horse's rump does the trick, or using light taps with a whip encourages the horse up the ramp – never beating, that only results in resistance. If the horse is really a challenge, a vet gives them a tranquilizer for the journey.

I had come in from a trail ride and saw three people struggling to get the horse loaded. Not wanting to get in the way, I sat on the horse I was riding and watched from the driveway.

This particular horse was stubborn. When they crossed the ropes behind him, he kicked out. They tried to encourage him with the whip and he responded by rearing. The more they tried, the more the horse acted up; fighting and refusing to get on the van. I watched them for a few minutes or so when I heard the yell.

"Get away from him!" the man yelled. "You're nothing but a bunch of amateurs!" Short, gray-haired, he marched toward the little group. Surprised, the three stopped. He grabbed the horse's lead line from one. From another, he took the whip and made as if to use it on them, scattering them away. He threw the whip to the ground, turned and walked up the ramp. The horse followed him like an obedient dog. No resistance, no balking.

He backed the horse in the stall and came out grumbling, "Bunch of amateurs!" He threw the lead rope in the direction of where the three were cowering and stalked back into the barn.

It didn't surprise me – I was prepared for what was coming after the yell. I'd been the target of his intimidating outbursts myself. Luckily, I felt I was in his good graces for the time being.

A riding stable is a kind of community where everybody knows everybody else – and frequently knows their personal business. I had been riding at Thorncroft for a few months and one evening stayed later than normal. A short, round man came in the barn carrying cardboard boxes and said, "John, move that horse over to another place. I want to use these cross ties."

"Yes, sir," John replied, jumping to quickly move the yearling he was grooming.

I was surprised to see easy-going John react like that and turned to watch the man with graying hair and trimmed beard walk down the aisle like he owned the place. I stood at the hallway leading to the lounge. He entered a stall in the boarder section of the barn and emerged leading a horse. He moved with conviction to the end of the barn and put the horse in the cross ties. One or two people passed by saying hello. He totally ignored them. He focused only on the horse.

A couple of young girls came out of the tack room and stood in the aisle to watch. They asked a few questions and got no response. The man continued to brush the horse's coat. They tried again. "Get out of here kids! Don't bother me, I'm working," he gruffly snapped.

They looked at each other and shuffled away.

Short and stocky, he had an imposing presence. I quietly moved away down the aisle.

I sought out John, who was putting hay in the stalls.

"Who is that guy?" I nodded towards the far end of the barn.

"Oh, him," John replied. "That's mean, old man Heffner."

"Why is he mean?"

"He lost his family in a fire. Keeps to himself now and doesn't have any friends."

I left John to his work in the stalls, and from a safe distance, watched the lone man at the end of the barn.

I began to see this mysterious man more frequently, but not every day. The barn at Thorncroft was long, with stalls lining the sides of a central aisle. I found excuses to hang out far enough away to not be noticed, yet close enough to keep an eye on Mr. Heffner and what he was doing.

Most everyone left him alone. He didn't respond to anyone anyway, even if they did try to talk with him. He usually arrived after most people had gone home. I didn't approach him either; just stood and watched from down the aisle. As often as I could stay late, I'd watch him with his horse. I'd station myself in the aisle pretending to be busy with something, but really just wanting a vantage point to observe. Sometimes he had to pass by me, but always looked straight ahead and never acknowledged me. He'd say hello to Mr. Dixon, the owner of the stables, but their conversations were short and concise, never very long.

Mr. Heffner always worked at the very end of the aisle. I didn't hang around watching too long, but I couldn't ignore him either. I felt sorry for him, having lost his family and not having any friends. He fascinated and scared me, and I wanted to know more about who he was.

Further inquiries of John revealed that Mr. Heffner took on difficult horses others didn't want to deal with or couldn't train. If a horse showed potential, but was hard to handle, they were sent to different trainers in the hopes that one would have the key to making the horse useful and easier to work with. If a horse was considered beyond hope, they'd sometimes be sent to the sales at New Holland in the Amish country.

New Holland is a borough in Lancaster County, Pennsylvania. The town's auction facility was old, with a large arena, fences, chutes, gates and dirt pens out back. Back then, buyers for pet food plants purchased sick, lame or unwanted animals. Many rundown horses unable to be helped ended up in the killer pens. Some owners, mostly unethical ones, who didn't want to pay the cost of vet bills to heal the horse or the expense of having him euthanized – or sometimes the parents of an unwanted backyard pony – sent their horses to New Holland as a quick, easy way to be rid of the animal and make a little money off it, too.

Horses, cattle, sheep, farm equipment, and tractor-trailer loads of hay and straw were auctioned every week. It was a warren of passageways and holding stalls. A shouted "heads up" would send everyone climbing up on the fence and out of the way of sheep or cattle being driven to or from the auction ring. When you said "New Holland" around horse barns, people knew you meant the horse sales. It was the end of the line for a lot of horses.

At times, a nice horse or pony could be found in the killer pens. Someone didn't know what they had and sold it cheap to the kill buyers. The kill buyers sometimes resold horses for their price plus a bit of profit. To do this, you had to know your way around horses. It was a risk not knowing why they were sent to New Holland in the first place.

There are stories of horses bought from the killers that went on to fame. The story of Snowman, the show jumper, is one such horse. In 1956, Harry de Leyer, a riding instructor from New York, saw a gray plow horse on one of the trucks going for slaughter. He was in the market for a lesson horse – one used to teach riding - and bought the gray for $80 and named him Snowman. He was a good lesson horse. Harry tried to sell Snowman, and each time he'd jump out of his new pasture and return to Harry. Harry finally decided to keep Snowman and train him as a show jumper. Snowman went on to a career in jumping and won many prestigious awards. He was inducted into the Show Jumping Hall of Fame in 1992. Three books on Snowman's incredible story have been written, as well as a film documentary made of his life.

In my quest to know more about Mr. Heffner, I found excuses to be in the barn when he was there. Little by little, I gathered up my courage and began to stand closer. It felt like slowly approaching a wild animal in a way that they wouldn't frighten and run off. Mr. Heffner never said anything to me.

Occasionally, he'd order someone out of his way. Everyone jumped when he said move. I never asked questions or said anything to him, just watched and stayed out of the way. One night he surprised me.

"What's your name, Kid?" he asked.

I told him, though I'm sure he already knew from Mr. Dixon. He asked me a few questions about school and my home. I was so ecstatic that he had talked to me. Each night I stood a little closer. He'd always ask me how I was doing. I ventured a few questions of my own. Some he answered, others he chose not to.

I gradually learned he had another family and had remarried sometime after the fire. His oldest daughter, from his first marriage, had been out of the house at the time of the fire. She was the only one to survive. He had three children with his new wife, two sons and a daughter.

*World in a Shoe*

*World in a Shoe*

## Chapter 10

# Your Hand On That Stall Door

I discovered that Mr. Heffner worked on other people's horses, the ones with problems such as lameness or behavioral issues. When I first met him, he was working with a large, black horse named Rasputin who had some kind of problem with his feet.

Over time, I learned he had taken on – with success – tough horses that other trainers had tried to work with and failed. I heard of two occasions where someone wanted to purchase a horse and the seller told them they also had to take a second horse, as they came together. Generally when this happened, they were trying to get rid of a problem horse and this was one way to do it. In both these cases, the "problem" horses turned out to be wonderfully nice horses, better than the ones they were sold with. Both these horses benefitted from Mr. Heffner's intervention.

When I was ten or so, Mom gave me the book, "Twenty Gallant Horses," by C. W. Anderson. I remember the dedication in the book as being "To James Rarey, the horse whisperer."

Horse whisperer was a term given to people at the turn of the century who had an uncanny ability to work with horses. It is said they whispered in the horse's ear and intractable horses became compliant.

One of the most famous of these was James Rarey, born in 1827. He took on some very difficult horses – man-killers, even – and was able to train them. In that era, horses were essential for commerce and travel. Every horse born had potential for use in riding, farm work and pulling carriages. Often, they were trained for more than one job.

Nowadays, horses largely are seen as a luxury and are often trained for one specific purpose or sport. They may get additional training later when they are unable to compete anymore. Training horses for an individual sport has become specialized, much like physicians in medicine. There are still some horses that are trained to be ridden and pull a carriage, but that is not the norm. When horses were used for virtually all kinds of transportation, a horse with a well-rounded education was desirable. Most people couldn't afford to purchase, let alone the upkeep, of one horse for riding and another to pull the carriage to church on Sundays.

No matter the temperament, they were put to use. It was imperative that difficult horses be trained to become useful animals, and there were trainers who specialized in working with these kinds of animals. If the horses couldn't be trained, they were sent to the killers.

From what I've researched, horse whisperers were secretive about their methods and insisted on working away from the prying eyes of the public. That was Mr. Heffner. Horses changed around him.

I discovered the cardboard boxes he brought into the stable from his car contained grooming supplies, equipment and bottles of liquids. He tested people – I didn't see until much later – including me. One night after he'd finished working with a horse and had gone home for the night, I found one of his mysterious little bottles left behind in the aisle. I figured he didn't want it laying around, so I locked it in my tack trunk until the next evening, when I returned it to him. He thanked me and didn't say anything more, but from that point on, he really began to teach me.

I don't remember how Mr. Heffner began teaching me. I'd hang around watching him and kept quiet. He'd ask questions. Then, little by little, he began to point things out to me.

Mr. Heffner was very exacting in how he worked with horses. He wanted things done a certain way and wouldn't tolerate it any other way. When he did talk, he said what he meant – bluntly overriding any objections from the listener. He wanted me to listen. He wasn't interested in what I thought I knew.

He knew my name, but always called me Kid. He seemed mysterious to me – a man of few words.

"Kid, the minute you put your hand on that stall door, you're horse training," he told me more than once. He was in teaching mode whenever he spoke with me or anyone else.

Early on, Mr. Heffner told me to read the book "King Solomon's Ring" by Konrad Lorenz. In it, I learned about anthropomorphism – the tendency to put human characteristics on animals. Many people want to see their pets as having human understanding and complex human emotions. Animals do have their own complex communications, just not what we were taught from children's books. Animals don't have cognitive thinking or the morals that humans have. They don't place meaning on things like we do.

As a child, I had read and been read to from books and watched TV programs where animals were portrayed as something like humans. It is very easy to fall into this way of thinking, that your dog or cat cares that you had a fight with your best friend and takes your side in the argument. Or to think your horse knows what your favorite color is. This isn't so. Animals have a complex set of intuitions and instincts that nature gave them to survive. The more domesticated they are, the more they learn to use their brain-mind to override the basic instincts.

Horses in nature don't normally accept things on their backs. It is a place where they can be vulnerable to attack from a predator, like a cougar leaping onto them from the branches of a tree. It is instinctive for a horse to try and throw off anything on their back. But they can learn to override this instinct and allow people to ride them.

I continued to read more books on animal psychology and training. Mr. Heffner often told me, "You never read to believe, only to weigh and consider." I don't remember the titles or authors, but I began experimenting with the information. One author wrote that animals communicate through mental images. They "feel" on a psychic, intuitive level and get the images. I've also heard this referenced in training dogs. When you want to teach a dog to sit, you hold an image of it sitting in your mind. It has to be a positive image – it is easier to visualize a dog sitting than not standing.

I decided to test this out when I went to the barn. The stable and indoor ring sat at the top of a hill near a large pasture. It was a short walk from the barn to turn horses out at the gate in the pasture, and a long walk through the pasture to catch a horse and bring it in for lessons unless the horses were up at the gate.

I went to the pasture and stood at the gate. The horses were down the hill and far out in the field in a couple of groups. I focused on one of the groups, sending them pictures of me standing at the gate. The horses stopped grazing, raised their heads and looked at me. I was surprised and tried it again, and again it happened. I tried to visualize them coming across the field to the gate. They didn't even raise their heads. I saw that something about it worked, but didn't yet understand how it applied to my day-to-day work with horses.

The horses usually are at the gate when it was feeding time, ready to come in for their grain. If it's not feeding time and they're way out in the pasture, the normal way to get most all of them to come in fast – as opposed to walking them in one by one – is to shake a metal bucket of grain by the gate and holler, "Come on!" A metal bucket works best, because the grain needs to make a sound the horses can hear. Yelling gets their initial attention, then your silhouette with the bucket and the sound of the grain is enough to cause them to trot and canter up for a treat. This was the way it was done on every farm I worked.

In later years, I began experimenting with the psychic aspect again. I'd carry a bucket to the gate and try variations of calling and/or sending out visions of grain.

The most effective method was calling once to get their attention, then sticking my nose in the bucket of grain and sending that sensation of yummy smell to the horses. They'd lift their heads and prick their ears at the first call, and after I'd smelled the grain, they began coming toward the gate. I was never able to get the horses to come without a bucket of grain.

## Chapter 11

# Take a Walk, Kid

Mr. Heffner only talked to the people he wanted to, and even then he kept them at a distance. As well as working with difficult horses, he had another skill he was known for in the wider horse world: bitting and floating horses' teeth.

Floating is a term used for a kind of filing down of the sharp edges of a horse's molars. The flat, rectangular, metal files used for this are called floats – hence "floating a horse's teeth."

The molars wear down from chewing grain, forming sharp edges. These edges can become so sharp that they slice the horse's cheeks and tongue. Sharp teeth can interfere with the horse's ability to chew, leading to digestive problems. They also can cause problems in riding. If a horse's mouth hurts, he won't be as responsive and cooperative to the rider's hands.

Floating the teeth removes these sharp edges. It needs to be done correctly so that none of the teeth are missed and the horse isn't injured in the process. Mr. Heffner floated horses' teeth as a business as well as the training he did.

Knowledgeable owners and trainers schedule a yearly exam of their horses' teeth for sharpness and floating. They check any new horse's teeth automatically.

Mr. Heffner was also an expert in bitting. The bit is the portion of the bridle that goes in the horse's mouth. It is usually made out of metal, but not always. Mr. Heffner had more bits than I'd ever seen before, even at tack shops.

Bits come in many varieties, from solid mouthpieces to two jointed or three jointed forms. They can be made of metal, steel, copper, vulcanite - a kind of hard rubber - and some bits are covered in softer rubber. The mouthpiece can be solid or hollow, thick or thin, plain or with rollers, and the side rings can be round, oval, D-shaped or with long, metal bars. Bits called snaffles work directly on the mouth, whereas a category called curb bits use leverage.

A horse may not use the same bit all the time. Some bits are used for a specific portion of the horse's training. For example, a young horse learning to steer from the rider's commands may need a full-cheek style of bit that puts a bit of gentle pressure on the side of his face to encourage him to turn. There are some horses that are so uncomfortable with a bit that they are ridden with a hackamore – a kind of bit-less bridle. People can abuse horses with the kinds of bits they choose. There are some schools of thought that decry the use of a bit at all.

Every horse's mouth is different and no one bit is good for all horses. There is a whole science and art to bits and bitting. Much of it relates to what the horse will be used for, his previous experience, training, personality, and even his bone structure and shape of his jaw. Mr. Heffner accounted for all these factors and more when working with a horse. I only had basic education in bits and bitting before I met him.

\* \* \* \*

Mr. Heffner worked his horses from the ground, lunging them on a long line in a circle. Or, he'd turn them loose - what's called "at liberty," where the horse moves freely in an enclosed arena.

He had a special apparatus he used on the horses called a bitting rig, which was a series of straps with a girth around the horse's middle. Some trainers use bitting rigs as part of a young horse's initial education. Bitting rigs are best used by experts. When used incorrectly, mistakes can lead to a horse being injured or even killed.

Mr. Heffner said his rig was different from ones you could purchase in tack shops. He'd learned about bitting rigs from some of his teachers and had designed parts of this one himself with specially made pieces. Mr. Heffner told me it connected a horse's mouth to his entire spine. "Kid, with this rig, a horse will teach himself," he said.

I didn't understand all that much at the time and if I asked too many questions, he'd cut me off with "Wouldn't you like to know!" If I tried to figure it out on my own and venture the answer, his quick, shouted response was, "Kid, you don't know what you're talking about. You don't know a thing!"

Mr. Heffner never hesitated to be direct. I'd never had anyone be that direct with me. If I was watching him work and someone came by he wanted to talk to, he'd say, "Take a walk, Kid. I need to discuss some business." It was refreshing compared to the strained silences of my home life.

He also helped me understand how to better interact with people. Growing up with my alcoholic mom was painful and confusing. I often didn't understand the signals I was getting from other people. They'd be friendly one minute and angry or aloof the next.

"It must be hard living with your mother, the way she is," he said once. "You don't always get the help you need."

We'd never spoken of my mother's drinking, but it didn't surprise me that he knew. The people around my mother rarely acknowledged her drinking. I see now that some of them had an agenda to keep her drinking because of her innate generosity. Mr. Heffner helped me understand how I made people angry with the things I said or did. Some of it I understood; some I had to grow into understanding as I got older. It was a mixed blessing. He had a temper that was hard for me to deal with, but his guidance was invaluable in those teen years.

*World in a Shoe*

## Chapter 12

# Talk is Cheap

It was clear to me Mr. Heffner knew more about horses than anyone I'd ever met before. I wanted to learn from him, but his temper was intimidating and he was demanding. He wanted me to do exactly as he said and often threatened to walk away and never talk to me again if I didn't. I was getting more and more attached to him, while at the same time growing intimidated. He was, in a way, acting as a father figure for my absent dad. I see now I was frightened of his anger and disapproval – and the possibility of losing him.

Mr. Heffner demanded obedience not only from me, but from the horses he worked with. He paid attention to the smallest details; things I thought were inconsequential often turned out to have a larger impact.

He insisted that a horse stand square on all four feet while he was working with it. From the moment he put a horse in the cross ties, even while taking breaks during training and grooming afterward, he made sure the horse was standing on all four legs.

If you've ever seen a horse at rest, you'll often notice it standing on one hind leg while cocking the other leg to rest on the toe. Mr. Heffner wouldn't let any of his horses do that. He told me, "Kid, don't ever let your horses cock a leg while you're grooming them. Always make them stand up in the cross ties." I asked why and he said, "I want the horse to pay attention to me while I'm working on it."

Over time, I formed a better understanding of why he did this. When you are working around a large animal with a finely tuned instinct for response, you want their attention in the present and on you. There's a better chance of maintaining control if something were to startle the horse. Additionally, it is a subtle reinforcement of hierarchy - you are training him to listen to you, even in small things.

Mr. Heffner was good with horses and hard on people. Things had to be exactly his way and he had very strong ideas about how people should be around horses.

"People think you can treat a horse like a pet, but you can't. You're only asking for trouble," he said many times. He wasn't unkind to the horses he worked with. On the contrary, he related to horses in their own form of communication – namely body language and understanding of herd hierarchy. He understood how horses interacted with each other and why they responded as they did. Years later, I could understand why he insisted on people doing exactly as he said when working with his horses. Horses are not pets and he spoke to this many times.

He also didn't stand for someone talking to their horse. "You're only going to confuse your horse if you try to talk to it," he told me.

Horses can learn word commands. People often teach them walk, trot and canter for lunging, but Mr. Heffner didn't use word commands when he longed his horses. He was mainly referring to people speaking with their horse, as if they could reason with it and the horse understood language.

He gave me an example of how a person could create confusion in the horse and not realize they were doing it. When training horses, people often pat or stroke them as a reward and to communicate they've done something correct. Then, while riding or leading the horse, if something spooks or upsets it, they stroke the horse to sooth it. Now the horse has learned that particular touch as a reward. Instead of getting the message to be soothed when nervous, the horse gets the idea that it's good and they should do more of that. "They inadvertently teach the horse the wrong thing," he told me.

Horses do communicate, much of it through body language. How a person physically, mentally and emotionally acted around a horse spoke volumes to him about that person and how they treated their horses.

Mr. Heffner was dubious of people's words as well. "Talk is cheap. Actions speak louder than words," he frequently told me. He never took anything written at face value, either. When something or someone felt off to him, he'd tell me, "Kid, I'm going to wait on this, watch, and see what happens." He found that giving things time and space often revealed more information.

Another of the basic things he did differently was to lead his horses from the off side. He had me do this whenever I led one of his horses. In horse lingo, the near side is the horse's left and the off side its right. In effect, the horse's head is to your right when you lead him. Most horses are trained to lead from the near side, and people are taught to do this as well.

I asked Mr. Heffner about it. He said he used the off side because it developed the other side of the horse's brain. "Everyone does everything from the near side. That only develops that side of the horse's brain," he said.

For me, it took some getting used to. His horses were all cooperative - they'd been doing this all along. Years later, while working jobs on horse farms, I still taught horses to lead from that side. Even though it wasn't the most frequent way they were led, I thought it was good training and flexibility for them to learn. It took a bit of persistence for the horses to get it, but eventually, they led equally well from either side. I also practiced mounting the horses from both sides so they'd be versatile in that, as well.

Whatever he did with a horse looked easy. I think that may be the comment I heard most often from people – he made it look so easy. He'd reply, "You just have to put a horse in a position to do what you want."

Economy of movement was important to him. "Don't make two trips when you can do it in one."

If he ever vacillated about something, I never saw it. "When you're doing something with a horse, do it with conviction. Don't pussy-foot around." When I didn't understand something he was telling me to do or was confused, he'd yell, "Stop pussy-footing around!" He wanted me to act in the moment. With a horse, quick timing can be everything. I just didn't have the gut-instinct to know what to do and would hesitate. That frequently got me in trouble with him. His yelling left me shaken.

Yet he knew so many things beyond the basic levels I'd been learning. Thorncroft had an indoor arena with lights, and some nights Mr. Heffner worked his horse there. But most nights he went out into the fields in the dark.

He didn't always tell me why he did the things he did, but one night he did. I asked why he worked his horses outside in the dark. "It teaches them to develop their other senses," he replied.

Whatever he taught me about horses I tried to apply to myself. Standing outside in the dark, where Mr. Heffner was working the horse, I could hear subtle changes in the sounds of the horse's hoof beats as he altered speeds.

Of course, once home at night, I ran around my neighborhood seeing if I could develop my hearing and other senses.

During this time I got my learner's permit to drive and eventually passed my driving test. I was able to drive to the barn on my own and stay as long as I wanted, no longer having to go when a friend's mother arrived to take us home.

\* \* \* \*

Mr. Heffner invited me to his house to meet his family - his new family. He had three children from his second marriage, the oldest of whom was around my age. They lived in one of the small, stone houses on the farm. He gave me a day and time to be there, and told me where to turn to find the house.

His wife, Dorothy, welcomed me and showed me into the kitchen amid barking, inquisitive dogs. Their daughter, Rachel, sat at the table. I learned they had two sons, Johnny and Michael, both of whom were out with friends. Johnny was the oldest and nearest to me in age, while Michael was in the middle and Rachel the youngest. Rachel and Mrs. Heffner rode, but the boys weren't interested in horses – at least in those years.

Mr. Heffner had a ritual. Every time he went into his house at the end of the day, he'd sit on a stool, remove his shoes and wipe the bottoms and sides of them with a rag dipped in a bucket of iodine solution he kept for that purpose. Then he'd slip into a pair of shoes or slippers to wear inside. He told me he went in different barns and places throughout the day and he didn't want to track all that dirt into his house. I took my shoes off and left them by the door.

"Dottie, get Nicole a plate," he said to Mrs. Heffner. "Stay and have some dinner," he told me. "I don't want you going home with a miss-meal cramp."

From then on, he often invited me to visit at a mealtime. After a few visits, I began to help with cleaning up and doing the dishes. At first he told me I didn't need to, but I felt strongly about it and he didn't say anymore.

After dinner, when the dishes were done, he'd start talking to me again about horses. Mrs. Heffner was in the den watching TV and the kids were upstairs or out with friends. We'd sit in the kitchen, and Mr. Heffner would bring a small desk lamp to the table and turn out the overhead light.

He had a small, red pocket notebook. He kept track of what training method he used for what horse, the kinds of equipment and bits he used, and the various homemade remedies and liniments for each horse, as well as how well they worked. He even made reminders to himself of the changes he'd advised a particular owner to make to improve their relationship with their horse.

He wrote down the ideas and insights that came to him. "Kid, when something comes to you, you need to write it down or you'll lose it," he told me. Many nights, I'd sit at his kitchen table with the desk lamp shedding a small circle of light and listen to him read me things from his little red notebook.

He had tiny writing and made notes in horse books he had in his library. They weren't the usual horse books that could be found in tack shops. They were old, cloth covered with yellowed pages. Sometimes he'd show me these. In many places, he had underlined the text and put stars in the margins – sometimes with cryptic letters or a word or two. Flipping to the back, he showed me the more complete set of notes he'd made on the blank sheet, with the page numbers for reference. Many of the notes had to do with horses he'd worked on or was currently working with.

I'd ask questions, and sometimes he'd answer. Most of the time, he'd tell me I didn't know a thing. I found I learned more by just being quiet and listening, even though I didn't understand a lot of what he was telling me.

While he had a wealth of knowledge, there were times he didn't have all the answers. He shared with me, "When you go to sleep at night, ask the Good Lord to bring you an answer to your problem. In the morning, you'll have your answer or some piece of information to begin to go on." He said it never failed for him.

I've used this on and off over the years. Most of the time I got some kind of an answer. The times that I didn't I chalked up to not remembering or in some way blocking the help. I'd keep asking each night until I got direction or an answer.

I was always amazed by his wealth of knowledge. Every time I sat with him, I learned something new. He'd chuckle and tell me, "Stick with me, Kid, and I'll make you famous."

When we were done for the evening, whether at the barn or in his kitchen, he'd say, "Kid, I'm going to leave you now, and that's more than the devil will do."

As I went out the door, he followed it up with, "Go straight home and stay out of the clubs." He knew I didn't go drinking – I wasn't really a party person. But it felt nice to have that little ritual.

*Chapter 13*

# It Doesn't Take Six Years

"I'm not going to tell you what to think. I'm going to teach you how to think," Mr. Heffner said numerous times. While he was teaching me, I thought he was imparting information to know and use. I later understood he was watching to see how well I put pieces of information together.

He said, "You never cover a horse's body that you don't also cover his legs." I wasn't sure exactly what he meant, but made a note of it. I knew people put blankets on their horses in the winter, especially if they clipped them. I knew a horse's legs were wrapped if he was injured and needed medication. Sometimes boots or wraps were used during competition and to protect their legs while shipping.

Perhaps a week or so later, he told me, "A horse doesn't have any muscle below his knee or hock. There's only bone, tendon, ligament, blood vessels, skin and the hoof." I thought there was a reason he was telling me this, but I didn't know why and made another note.

A few days after that, sitting in his kitchen, he told me about a show horse he had taken care of. The horse had a habit of breaking out – sweating after he'd been exercised and cooled off. A horse that continues to break out can lose condition and in cool weather become chilled.

Mr. Heffner told me that when the horse came into his care, he covered the horse's legs whenever he put a blanket on him. The sweating stopped. He asked me why that would be. I had no idea. He reminded me that a horse has no muscle in his lower legs. The blood moving though the lower legs cooled off too quickly because the vessels were close to the skin, and therefore more exposed to the cold air. A horse's body had to work to warm it up again. The horse wasn't cooling off completely, and this caused him to break out again. Wrapping the horse's legs kept the blood at a more even temperature, allowing him to cool off completely and stay dry.

I never would have put that together without his help. But this is the way in which he tried to teach me. He'd give me a piece of information, then wait awhile and give me something else and see how long it took me to put the pieces together. I'm sure I missed much of what he wanted me to see, but it did begin to change the way I looked at the world.

Mr. Heffner had all these little bits of wisdom he'd occasionally share. He once told me that "You can make a horse that is too strong on the bit more compliant by weaving a little of his tail hair in the curb chain." When I asked why this worked, he said he didn't know, but had learned it from a Native American.

"God gave animals the ability to know what they need for their own healing, Kid," he said once. "Some afternoon, follow the horses in the pasture and watch what they eat." He told me to pay attention to what plants the horses grazed on. All of them would eat some plants such as grasses. Other types of plants, only one or two of the horses would choose.

He continued, "Horses and animals close to nature have an inner knowing of what their body needs for healing."

I followed the horses in the field and watched what they ate. Like he said, they nibbled on different plants. I don't know if he meant for me to do it, but I tried a little of each plant I saw the horses eat. Some were grassy and others bitter. It was interesting to see what they wanted.

"Kid, it doesn't take six years, six months, six weeks, six days or six hours to teach a horse. A horse can learn something in six minutes," he'd say. When he got a horse to do something he wanted, he'd reward them and then step back to stand or sit on a stool a few feet away, keeping a light hold on the rope. "People don't realize that a horse needs time to process when they are learning. They keep giving the horse input – petting and talking to him, trying to do the next thing. The horse gets confused and doesn't know what you're trying to teach him." He showed me how to hold the rope to keep a light contact, but to give the horse space. "You just need to give him six minutes to take in what you've just done and he'll start putting it together." Like with me, he was giving the horse time to put it together.

He had his own way of doing things that weren't standard in the horse world. Once, when I said I had to leave early to feed my horses, he told me I should keep a looser schedule. "If you always feed at the same time each day, a horse's internal clock gets set to that time. Then if you're late for some reason, they can get anxious, and that can cause upset digestion. Say you feed at five o'clock in the afternoon. Start by feeding a little earlier on some days or a little later on others. Vary it each day – up to twenty minutes or so. That way your horses know you're coming somewhere in that time frame and they don't get anxious." It was obvious once he explained it to me.

Mr. Heffner helped many people and their horses. Rarely was it a problem with the horse. Mostly, it was the people who didn't know or understand how to work with their horse. They met with his ire like I did.

He was often cryptic when teaching and I didn't always understand, but I learned early on about conjecturing or voicing what I thought I knew. "You think you know so much. You don't know anything - you're just a rank amateur!" He'd shout. It irked him when someone tried to impress him that they knew things when they really didn't.

Sometimes he wouldn't say anything to me for the rest of the visit until it was time to go home. He had a flash temper. If I didn't get what he meant, I stayed quiet, hoping to eventually come to some understanding of what he'd been saying.

It was frustrating, and at times, infuriating. I tried to talk back on occasion to explain that I didn't understand. But he was louder and more forceful, and I always backed down. There were times I was furious, and then I'd fall into the fear that I'd lose him if I made him mad enough.

## Chapter 14

# The Chestnut Pony

"Seventy-five percent of horses will train themselves," Mr. Heffner told me, "but the other twenty-five percent you have to know what you are doing." His daughter Rachel's horse, Kiowa, had been one of those problem horses. The Pinto mare was now so well-behaved that Rachel did back somersaults off Kiowa's hindquarters. I saw her do this many times.

One of the horses Mr. Heffner had taken on was a small, reddish pony he named The Chestnut Pony. Though he was a pony, he was not typical. His presence lent him the stature of a larger horse. Muscled and rounded, he reminded me of the horse in George Stubb's 1762 painting "Whistlejacket."

"Chestnut" because that's the name for horses of that color; "Pony" because he was exactly 14.2 hands high - the official size of a pony. Horses are measured in "hands" from the ground to the top of the withers, just behind where the neck joins the back. Each hand is four inches. Anything above 14.2 hands is considered a horse.

In shows, classes for horses and ponies are usually separated; the jumps for horses being higher than those for ponies. Because of their size, ponies can be good for kids learning to ride. A good, well-trained pony is invaluable for a child to learn on.

The Chestnut Pony demonstrated one of the most genuine displays of happiness and joy in a horse I ever saw. Horses can be exuberant, running, bucking and playing when you turn them out. One afternoon, walking down the aisle of the barn, I saw The Chestnut Pony jumping and making little squealing noises in his stall. Then he stood still, facing in the direction of the driveway with his head raised, ears pricked forward. After a bit, he began jumping again. He did this two or three times.

I saw Mr. Heffner's car come in the driveway. I realized he recognized the sound of Mr. Heffner's car approaching. He hadn't always been this happy.

The Chestnut Pony was one of those horses considered difficult to work with. He had been sent around to different trainers in the area, but no one seemed able to do anything with him. Mr. Heffner took him on.

He usually worked with The Chestnut Pony at night after the day's lessons were done and most everyone had gone home.

"Come here, Kid, I want to show you something about The Chestnut Pony," Mr. Heffner called me to come closer. He had him on the cross ties at the end of the barn. He worked his hand into The Chestnut Pony's mouth and held it open. He was an expert with his hands in a horse's mouth because of his years floating teeth. "Look in there. Do you see his tongue? Do you see that scar on it?"

I did see it – a large diagonal scar that creased the tongue back by the molars. He said, "Someone really hurt him with a bit and put a deep cut in his tongue."

He led me around behind the horse and said, "Now, look at his hindquarters and tell me what you see." At first I didn't see anything. "You're not looking right!" he exclaimed and went on, "Look at the point of his hips. What do you see?" The point of a horse's hip is where the pelvis juts out. Normally, the hindquarters are fairly evenly rounded and balanced. There can be some differences. Like people being right- or left-handed, horses can be one-sided. I looked at The Chestnut Pony's hips and saw the right side was rounded and the left was sort of concaved in a few inches. The left was not symmetrical with the right.

"Sometime in his past, he broke the point of his hip," Mr. Heffner told me. It wasn't a glaring difference and it wasn't noticeable from the side. You only saw it when looking directly from behind. He told me the important thing was with the old break healed in this position, The Chestnut Pony's back was affected.

"He doesn't have the muscle to carry a rider properly. And he's afraid of his mouth being hurt again. If someone didn't know what they were looking at with this horse, they'd be in trouble."

The good news was Mr. Heffner knew how to help The Chestnut Pony. He explained he was teaching him to use different muscles to compensate for the weakness on the one side.

The Chestnut Pony was one of those horses bursting with life and energy. Mr. Heffner worked him at liberty in the ring and he trotted, cantered, turned on a dime and leapt tall jumps on command. He even got so he could be ridden.

I rode him a few times. It was like sitting on a living wave of powerful effervescence. He was unlike any horse I'd ever been on. His strides were bouncy, even his walk. He was very sensitive to any kind of touch – especially in his mouth. He was what is termed "light as a feather."

He was more horse than I could handle. It was hard to admit it then, but I don't mind saying it now.

*World in a Shoe*

*World in a Shoe*

## Chapter 15

# The Kokomo Kid

Mr. Heffner sometimes referred to The Chestnut Pony as The Kokomo Kid. I'd never heard the expression and asked about it.

"Have you ever heard of Kokomo, Indiana?" he replied. I hadn't. "It's a small town, not any big shots come from there. It's an expression we used at the track." It meant that a horse had potential and was expected to be big.

"When the horse went for his morning gallop, someone'd call out, 'There goes the Kokomo Kid!' We'd all stand at the door to watch him go by," he said.

Training and floating teeth weren't the only things Mr. Heffner did. He had homemade remedies for healing horses. He kept cardboard boxes loaded with gallon milk jugs and plastic squeeze bottles in the trunk of his car. These jugs and bottles were filled with mysterious liquids of different colors and consistencies.

He told me he'd learned a lot from a veterinarian, Dr. Ed Caslick. He spoke of him often with tremendous respect, and some of the remedies he used were from him.

People, as well as horses, could use most of the remedies Mr. Heffner made. They always asked him what was in the remedies. "Wouldn't you like to know!" he'd say. He'd mix up batches by the gallon and sell them to his customers. Though they didn't know what was in them, they bought them anyway because they worked. I was curious, and of course, asked what was in them. He said the same thing to me as he said to everybody else.

Some remedies were liniments, others were for healing. One in particular had many uses – one of which was diagnosing inflammation. Then there were the tonics.

He made a standard tonic. He liked to make people drink it and watch their reactions. One time he gave me a small glass of it. The tonic was intense. I tasted vinegar and something sweet, like molasses, and it made me cough.

He laughed. "That'll put hair on your chest, Kid." He instructed me to, "Stir it in their feed with your hands." The horses loved it. "It'll put dapples on a horse's coat," he said. Like Mr. Heffner said, their coat improved and the dapples appeared.

The tonics and remedies remained a mystery to me for many years. Probably the most famous one Mr. Heffner was known for was Sweet Talk, and he was never without a small, cone-tipped bottle of it. Thick and viscous, it looked like molasses. "It's not molasses, Kid, but something entirely different," he said. "It feeds the horse's brain." He used it by squeezing a bit into the corner of the horse's mouth.

"I got this formula from an animal trainer with the Ringling Brothers, Barnum and Bailey Circus," he told me. I believed it - all the animals at the barn seemed to like it. I saw him give it to dogs and even cats. They were always ready for more. Even now, when I think of the Sweet Talk, I imagine someone giving it to a big tiger.

He shared with me a story. One time, he was using his remedies to help someone with a horse. He drove out to the farm where they were boarding it a few times a week. He was having success and the people there were curious, but he knew some of them "were up to no good." They wanted to get hold of his remedies, have them tested and see what was in them.

He devised a plan – he carried a gallon milk jug back and forth to the barn. The jug didn't have a remedy in it – he had filled it with water and food coloring. The real remedies he hid with his other things. Every day, when no one was looking, he'd pour a little of the colored water out in the corner of the stall. "They could see the level in the jug going down," he said. One day he left the bottle locked in the back seat of his car while he worked the horse.

"Sure enough, the window was broken and they'd stolen the jug out of the car. Imagine their surprise when they found it was only food coloring and water," he chuckled at the memory.

\* \* \* \*

"I may not always be right, but I'm never wrong!" he laughed. I had been riding The Chestnut Pony and thought I was doing well.

We were at a medium trot in the arena when Mr. Heffner called out, "I've told you before to keep a soft fist on the reins." I thought I was doing that, but then he angrily yelled, "Close the ring finger of your left hand!"

Startled, I looked down and saw that, sure enough, the ring finger on my left hand was about half an inch more open than the others. I closed my finger. "That's it!" he said.

*"How the heck could he see that?"* I thought. I'd seen him squinting over his notes in the evenings. I couldn't figure out how he could have seen my finger from all the way across the arena.

I later asked how he could see my hand. He told me he didn't need to see my hand. He could tell what was going on by the way The Chestnut Pony was moving. He chuckled, "Only God's right a hundred percent of the time, but I'm right ninety-eight!"

Horses seemingly changed shape around him. I once saw him walk up to a horse with a bit of a sway back. As he approached, the horse lowered its head and rounded its back. It looked like an entirely different animal. He had never worked with this horse before. The owner had asked Mr. Heffner to take a look at his teeth.

He paid attention to small details and made extra efforts with the horses in his care. I was learning that each horse needed to be treated differently. Mr. Heffner went out of his way to give a horse any special attention it required to be at its best. He told me of times he worked with show horses.

"Some horses get bored being in their stalls so much and they can start to get anxious," he said. "Some of us grooms would take them out in the afternoons to walk around and graze – sometimes two or three times." They did this even after the horses had been exercised. He told me it made a world of difference to the horse's outlook and happiness.

He knew how horses think and relate to the world around them. "A change of direction is a change of mind," he often said, meaning if a horse was resisting or not paying attention, to change direction – ride in a circle or across the arena. Changing direction would often put the horse in a different frame of mind. It seemed like simple advice, but I often saw riders continuing to go around the edge of the arena struggling with their horse.

Mr. Heffner knew about conformation, the basic bone and body structure of horses. Conformation is what made them athletic or not, good jumpers or not. The slope and angle of the shoulder and hindquarters, the length of their neck and the proportions of their legs had everything to do with how well a horse could perform. It also impacted how well he stayed "sound" – not going lame or getting injured. Years later, he helped me understand this with a buckskin mare I owned. She and I had a great connection, but because of the conformation of her front legs she was never going to be that great over fences. She was wonderful for trail riding – nothing spooked or surprised her.

Mr. Heffner and I attended horse seminars as spectators, and he'd quiz me on what I saw and then point out something I had missed. He'd comment on things about the horses or riders he wanted me to pay attention to. One time he said, "Watch the horse's tail as he trots down the long side – see how the bottom of it sways more to the right than to the left. The horse isn't engaging his near hind leg as much." The horse may have been stiff on that side or the rider may not have been using that leg as much as the other.

When I first read about horse whisperers, I imagined they performed some sort of magical spell on a horse. Mr. Heffner knew a lot that was practical, but he could also affect horses without touching them. At one seminar, we were sitting in the observation section behind a low wall. The teacher was in the center of the arena.

"Watch this, Kid," Mr. Heffner said.

He began to make low noises only I could hear and gesture with his fingers, making circular movements out of sight by his side. Every horse that passed by turned his head and watched Mr. Heffner - no matter what the rider was telling them to do. This was also much to the consternation of the man teaching the seminar, he remonstrated the riders needed to have better control of their horses.

I once saw Mr. Heffner put a horse into a trance-like state. He was floating the horse's teeth and had stopped for a break. Standing on one side of the horse's head, he began to gesture about six inches above the horse's face and make soft noises – the same noises he made at the seminar. The horse began to lower its head. The atmosphere grew still and silent. I was quietly standing nearby, not moving a muscle. I simply swallowed. The horse's ears flicked at the sound and his head popped up.

"You just broke the spell," Mr. Heffner said. He wasn't mad. I had no idea something so small as the sound of a single swallow could have that effect.

Not every sound he made was linked to something mysterious with a horse. When I had first started hanging around, hoping to learn from him, I noticed he made a whistle-like noise through his teeth when he groomed his horses. One day, I screwed up my courage and asked him why he whistled like that. Did it have some special effect on the horse?

"Oh, that," he laughed. "I whistle like that so the dust doesn't blow in my mouth while I'm brushing them."

*World in a Shoe*

*Chapter 16*

# I Knew It Was Horses for Me

Mr. Heffner was a character. I tried to get him to tell me about his background with horses, and sometimes he shared pieces – often late in the evening, under the light of a small lamp at the kitchen table.

He was born and grew up in Philadelphia with his mother and siblings. He never spoke of his father being around. He had a couple of brothers and sisters, the youngest, being Aunt Betty, who I got the chance to meet a few times.

He spoke repeatedly of a few men he'd learned from. In addition to Dr. Ed Caslick, he spoke of Walter J. Briggs. "He trained horses at a livery stable. I saw things you wouldn't believe. He could make a horse canter backwards," he said, shaking his head at the memory.

He frequently mentioned that he learned this or that piece of knowledge from Chief Red Eagle. I had the impression he'd traveled around the country, working different horse jobs, learning volumes at each place.

I knew he'd worked with show horses. I found out about his experience with racehorses when he told me the way to keep water from sloshing out of a barrel was to float a block of wood in it. One of his jobs was to accompany racehorses from one track to another. Before vans and air travel were common, horses traveled mostly by train. "In the boxcar," he said, "there was a large wooden barrel with the top open. It was filled with water, and we'd use that to water the horses. With the movement of the train, water would slosh out if we didn't put a block of wood in it."

*World in a Shoe*

As a young man, he had worked with polo ponies in the Northeast. I knew from what he'd told me about the Sweet Talk's formula that he'd had some exposure to the circus, though I never found out whether he worked there or not. He had experience with American Saddlebreds as well as hunter show horses.

Mr. Heffner also served in World War II. "I wanted to be in mule regiment," he told me. "They used mules to move cannons around." Instead he was assigned to a different unit that fed troops in the field. "In the end, I was glad I wasn't with the mule unit. They got bombed pretty badly and I wouldn't have wanted to see it," he said.

One night I asked him how he got interested in horses in the first place.

"I used to run with a pack of kids roaming the city - we'd be out all day," he said. "Sometimes we'd go down to the armory where the ships dock." He explained some of the ships were military, and in those days the army still had mounted cavalry units. The ships carrying the horses docked so they could take the horses off for exercise, bringing twenty-five or so horses out at a time.

"They'd run a rope through all the halters and tie it to the end horse. A rider on the front horse took hold of the rope and led them through the streets at a trot." He mused for a minute, then continued. "This one day I was there with a group of kids, and one of them dared me to jump on the back of the last horse in the line. So I did. I ran and jumped on. From that moment forward, I knew it was horses for me."

*Chapter 17*

# Morven Park

I attended a summer riding program at Morven Park International Equestrian Institute in Leesburg, Virginia, after my junior year of high school. I was still taking regular lessons as well as learning from Mr. Heffner. A couple of the instructors at Thorncroft were Morven Park graduates. They encouraged us to go there even for a short course in the summer.

Horse cavalry units were part of most militaries until they mechanized during World War II. When the horse units were disbanded, some of the cavalry officers went on to teach at riding schools to impart the knowledge they had. Major Lynch, a British cavalry officer, was the primary and best-known teacher at Morven Park. Major Lynch was no longer at the school the summer I attended and classes were taught by some of the graduate teachers.

Set in the rolling hills of rural Virginia, the Morven Park Equestrian Center was part of an old estate. When I went, the school offered summer programs and a longer, nine-month program. The facility had indoor and outdoor arenas, barns, a cafeteria and a lecture room. In addition to dorm cottages, there was the option to share a townhouse in Leesburg with other students, which I did.

The students maintained and cared for the horses – mucking stalls, feeding and watering. We swept the barn and cleaned our tack. Unlike lesson barns, where each horse has its own saddle and bridle, we were given a list of tack to bring. The school required a Fulmer snaffle and also a double bridle – a kind with two bits. Though I'd read about double bridles, I'd never worked with it or the Fulmer snaffle.

It was my first exposure to Three-Day Eventing, a kind of triathlon for horses. It was good, all-around training for horse and rider. Three-Day Eventing came out of the training given for military horses. Day one is Dressage and demonstrates the horse's obedience to the rider. Day two is cross country, showing the horse's endurance and flexibility over a cross country course that includes obstacles in natural settings: bank jumps, water jumps, ditches and fences at unusual angles. The riders and horses were expected to take the best line with each obstacle, jump without hesitation and continue on. Show jumping comprised the third day, which demonstrated the horse's continued fitness and ability after two days of tough competition.

The Morven Park instructors gave us a great foundation for understanding the sport. In addition to riding, we had sessions in the classroom each afternoon. We learned about all kinds of things, such as different hays and grains, stable management, and first aid for horses and riders. The information was at a very detailed level. I remember one lecture about what happens at a cellular level from injury to healing. I gained a new vocabulary from that lecture, including words like fibroblasts and lymph system. I also had an understanding of why swelling occurs and why icing an injury has the effect that it does. Outside the classroom, we had practical lessons where we learned how to apply different kinds of bandages correctly and hands-on first aid.

One of the most valuable things I learned at Morven Park, and I applied to every barn I worked at afterward, was fire prevention and how to set up an evacuation plan. We were taught to inspect the areas of the barn that could be vulnerable to fire.

It was important to have an evacuation plan in place ahead of time. It's too late to try and figure out what to do once a barn has caught fire. Everyone who worked at the barn needed to know the plan and to occasionally review it.

The best option is to never have a fire, of course; yet if it happens, you want to have a good plan in place. It sounds like common sense, but over the years it surprised me to discover many riding stables didn't have a fire plan.

The days passed quickly at Morven Park and I enjoyed the discipline of the schedule and a well-run stable. One of my favorite things was something called drill rides. With as many as twenty riders in the arena, we split into two teams called files. Our instructor called out directions and the two files circled and interwove with each other. You had to have control of your horse and maintain the proper distance from the rider in front of you to avoid a collision. Not only did you need to keep the right distance, you also had to watch the leader for the signal when to turn so everyone moved in unison.

As well as learning to ride drills, we also learned to direct them. You had to stay a few steps ahead of the riders in your head and plan the next movements to avoid chaos. It was challenging and a lot of fun. You learned to multitask – control your horse, maintain distance, watch the file leader and listen to the instructor. Years later, when I was teaching, I did mini-drill rides at walk and trot with my students.

I had my first experience of jumping chutes at Morven Park. Jumps were set up at intervals along the long wall of the arena. Poles and jump standards were set up on the inside to create a guide fence. We cantered the horses through the chute, jumping each fence in succession. When we jumped, we left our reins knotted on the horse's neck while holding our hands out to the sides, or we went through the chute, reaching forward to touch our toes at each jump – right hand to right toe and left hand to left toe. Sometimes we jumped through without stirrups or reins. Though we didn't do it on our course, I heard about students going through the chute taking off and putting on their riding jackets.

One of the first lessons we learned at Morven Park was how to open, walk through and close a gate from the back of a horse. It was more efficient than getting off and then back on again. We used this to enter and exit the indoor arena and also on the days we took the horses on walking hacks.

On one of the weekend days, we rode the horses for long, leisurely walks of an hour or so. We were only supposed to walk, as it was a kind of rest day for the horses. Going out in groups of three or four, we were left to our own devices. We'd wander all over the fields and trails of the estate. Large tracts were fenced for cattle grazing. We'd ridden through these areas before during lessons on cross-country riding. On walking days, we used the gates to move between fields.

One of the instructors had an Irish setter, and one day it followed three of us on a hack into the cattle pasture. The dog was running around chasing through the underbrush and disappeared into some large bushes, barking furiously. The bushes started shaking and moving. The dog shot out of the bushes at a full run with a very agitated bull on its heels. It streaked straight for us. We were already heading for the gate and realized we'd have to go faster than a walk if we were going to get away safely. We took off at a canter and jumped over the logs in the fence line. It was scary, but we were laughing at the close call and never told anyone we did more than walk that day.

The summer at Morven Park felt like it ended too soon. When the course was over, I headed back to Pennsylvania, inspired and eager. I learned so many things I wanted to put to use in my riding.

## Chapter 18

# Explain

Upon returning to the farm after the summer course at Morven Park, I thought I knew a lot about horses and was finally getting somewhere. Now a teenager, I was rebellious and on a mission to prove something. Mr. Heffner continued to prove how little I actually did know. His angry outbursts were more and more frequent.

One evening I was helping him unload his car. "Put that box right there in the aisle," he said. I reasoned that if I put the box in the middle of the aisle where he said, one of us might trip over it. So I set it to one side.

He roared, "I didn't tell you to put the box over there! If I wanted the box over there, I'd have said to put it over there!" He continued to rant at me for a good ten minutes, even after I moved the box back to the middle of the floor. He kept on that I was an amateur and didn't know a thing, threatening once more to walk away and not ever talk to me again.

His temper was getting harder and harder for me to handle. He was exacting of his horses and demanded it of me as well. Even in our talks in his kitchen, he didn't let up. A typical conversation went something like:

"How was the horse show, Kid?" he asked after I'd gone to watch a local horse show one weekend.

"It was good," I replied.

"What was good about it?"

"There were some nice horses at the show."

"Explain," he said.

"I saw a gray horse I liked," I replied.

"Why did you like it?"

"I thought it had good conformation."

"What was good about its conformation?"

I went on to explain some things about the horse's front legs I thought were good. He demanded details, and if he thought I was off about something, he'd tell me in no uncertain terms. These sessions felt more like interrogations than conversations and left me exhausted.

All of this pressuring for detail did have a purpose, which I discovered years later working on a horse with an injured leg. Mr. Heffner had given me some of his healing remedies and said he'd take me through the process of how to apply them. "Kid, I'm going to let you do the work. I won't lay a hand on the horse. I won't even lay eyes on him."

There were a number of steps to the process, first was determining where the inflammation was. When you can't see the inflammation, you can feel it by its heat. One of the remedies he called a wet pack assisted in this. He told me, "Put this on from the top of the withers down to the hoof, and then feel for heat." Sure enough, the horse had intense heat other places than the injured knee.

"Just tell me where the heat is - not where you think it should be or want it to be, but where it is," he said. He had me describe, inch-by-inch on the horse's leg, where I found heat.

"Was it the same amount of heat on the inside of the joint as on the outside? How much more? Did the heat go all the way up the tendon or just a little bit?" Every evening I stopped by and gave my report, and he told me what to do next.

The horse got better, and though its racing days were over, it went on to have a productive life beyond the track.

Riding lessons with Mr. Heffner were getting harder and harder as well. I had growing resentment of his constant insistence that I do everything exactly as he said. There was no room for me to misunderstand or ask questions, and very little room to make mistakes.

If I didn't understand something and tried to clarify it, he'd get even louder, "Just do as I say and stop pussy-footing around!"

His angry outbursts were more frequent. I wanted Mr. Heffner to acknowledge I had improved, that I knew a few things about horses. In reality, I wasn't as good a rider as he wanted – and needed to be – for the horses he was training, and I couldn't accept that. "You're a rank amateur, Kid. You think you know so much – well you don't." When I tried to tell him I did know something, he'd shout even louder. Underneath it all, I still wanted his approval.

He shouted when I made mistakes. I got nervous and made more until he was yelling at me to get off the horse. More than once I left our session in tears. He couldn't abide crying.

The evenings in his kitchen were better, but sometimes he'd continue to pound on me about all the things I'd done wrong. I was a teenager, rebellious, and getting angrier and angrier. I wanted to show him he couldn't boss me around like that. In hindsight, I saw that I really wanted to not be so afraid of him.

One afternoon I was riding The Chestnut Pony. Mr. Heffner yelled that I was doing everything wrong. His instructions sounded contradictory to me. He'd tell me to make a turn and when I did, he yelled that I wasn't listening. I was upset and The Chestnut Pony started rearing. He yelled for me to get off the horse. I started to tell him I didn't understand, but he roared over me, saying he didn't want to hear my excuses and that I must be some kind of imbecile to not understand. I got angry. I don't remember what I said, something along the lines of my not being good enough for him, and that no one was. I refused to cry again in front of him. I'd had enough. I handed him the reins and stormed off.

It was a long time before I spoke to him again. I was going to prove not just to Mr. Heffner, but to myself that I didn't need him, that I could do just fine and learn without his yelling and criticism.

Yet some people are in our lives for reasons beyond what we know. I did reconnect with him at a time when I lost myself and the things I held dear, and he gave me the guidance I needed.

*World in a Shoe*

## Chapter 19

# Porlock Vale in England

One of the boarders at Thorncroft was a professional artist. She encouraged me to do more with my art. I applied to and attended Philadelphia College of Art, but only for a year before the pull of horses lured me back.

The time away deepened my desire to make horses my vocation as well as my avocation. I decided my art was secondary.

I didn't return to Thorncroft. Instead, I went to Phoenixville, Pennsylvania, and met new riding instructor, Lorie.

I don't remember where I got the idea to attend the Porlock Vale riding school in England - maybe Lorie brought it up. When I was younger, I avidly read the book "The Horsemasters" by Don Sanford. Walt Disney also produced a movie by the same name. Both the book and movie were based on Porlock Vale Equitation Center in Somerset, England, on Bristol Bay. The school offered the British Horse Society's Assistant Instructor Certificate. My mom supported my changing desires and agreed to let me go to England.

Porlock was a world away. It wasn't the first time I'd been out of the country, or on my own for that matter. But it was the first time I'd be on my own while out of the country.

Like Morven Park, Porlock Vale was set up so the students took care of the horses as well as learned about riding. Upon acceptance to the course, we were given a list of required clothing. In addition to the usual riding breeches, boots and jacket, the list called for a uniform for stable work: blue jeans, Wellingtons, light blue long-sleeved shirts, a navy blue V-necked sweater and a navy blue bandana that served as a headscarf.

Instead of stock ties or chokers, women wore a man's tie – so I learned how to tie one. In a way, it was easier to only have these simple sets of clothes to look after. We washed them by hand in the laundry room and hung them to dry on lines. A blessing was the small, electric spinner in the corner.

A squared-off muckheap. Anyone who's been through a course at Porlock remembers this. In the United States, manure and dirty straw from the stalls are dumped in a pile away from the barn. Every few weeks, a large tractor-trailer with a claw comes to collect the manure and take it away.

At Porlock, the manure pile, called a muckheap, was given special attention. We were instructed on how to do this properly. The manure wasn't simply piled on. Every morning after stables, we turned out with pitchforks, rakes and brooms to "set fair" the muckheap. The manure was spread around evenly and packed down by beating it firmly with pitchforks. And not just in any shape – it had to be a rectangle with even sides, the walls perfectly straight and squared corners. Each day it grew higher. When the heap got taller than we could climb onto easily, we would stick pitchforks into the sides to make a kind of stairs. We raked the sides and swept all around. At the end of every session, it looked like a flat-topped shed covered in brown shag carpet.

Compacting the straw and manure in this way generated a lot of heat, which helped it break down more quickly. It was also warm on your feet in the rubber Wellies when you were up top.

Years later, working at a farm, I started keeping a squared manure pile. Our manure was sent to the mushroom farms in the area. The manure collection people were impressed when they came to gather it, but they asked I not do it again. Everything was breaking down too fast from the heat for them to use it.

Porlock was a collection of stalls in groupings on the property, called yards. I was assigned to Top Yard and had two horses to look after. Our day began with morning stables, the care and feeding of the horses, and cleaning their stalls. The stable manager measured out each horse's specific portion of grain, which we then took to the stalls. A special wheelbarrow with large holes drilled in it was used for wetting hay. Hot water was poured over the hay flakes, which emitted a fragrant steam in the early dawn air. They were allowed to sit until they were cool enough for the horses to eat.

Once morning stables was finished, we went to the dining room for our own breakfast. When breakfast was done, we had riding lessons and stable management lectures. A large focus on the course was learning how to conduct riding lessons, to assess the strengths and weaknesses of students, and to ask them for more, but not too much. We learned to progress students through different levels so they gained confidence in themselves.

Bones of some of the old Porlock horses were displayed in the lecture room. A skull from one horse showing all the teeth sat on the table, and on the side stood the leg bones and hoof from another. Some of the instructors knew these horses when they were alive and shared some stories with us. It may sound gruesome, but it was a kind of honor the horse continued to teach through its remains.

The farrier didn't come to the school to shoe the horses – we took the horses to him. It was a short ride into the town of Porlock. Every once in a while, instead of doing morning stables, two or three of us took horses to the blacksmith. Dressed in breeches, boots, jackets and riding hats, we rode the country roads into town. We'd leave the horses with the blacksmith and walk across the street to have tea and scones while waiting.

When I came back to the States just before Christmas, 1976, I was offered the job of head riding instructor and stable manager of a small, but busy stable in the Chester Springs area of Pennsylvania.

*World in a Shoe*

*Chapter 20*

# More Frightened Than Aggressive

Lorie, my riding instructor before Porlock, had moved on and I took over her position with the stable.

The farm had a barn with twelve stalls and an out building with two additional stalls. At any given time, there were roughly twelve to fourteen horses there. A couple were privately owned and not used at all for lessons. The rest were either owned by the stable or on "lesson board" - privately owned and used for teaching.

We only had an outdoor arena and small pasture. Most of the riding and lessons took place from spring, when it began to thaw, and lasted through fall and the freezing weather. I mostly taught children, though I had a few adult students, too.

I ran a summer riding camp for the young students. Their parents dropped them off in the mornings and I'd have them for three or four hours. They had lessons in the ring, as well as many facets of horse care. They learned about feed, hay, first aid and how to clean and take proper care of the tack.

As with most stables where lessons are taught, there are teenagers who come to the barn every day just to be around the horses. They come after school and in the summer all day long. If they wanted to hang out, we put them to work helping with grooming, taking care of tack and getting the horses ready for lessons. The older barn kids were an invaluable asset – they got to know each horse and could see the early signs if one was not well.

Along with the boarders, sometimes people sent us horses for a month or so for some training. A famous trainer – not Mr. Heffner – sent an Appaloosa gelding that was for sale. Friends of his wanted one of my students, a friend of theirs, to buy the horse. He was a terrifically nice horse and would have been a good match for my student – the only problem was he was a little lame. It wasn't an obvious limp, mostly showing up while he trotted downhill and on a curve. It was so slight that on the straight he looked sound. His lameness could have been due to something as inconsequential as a small sprain that would get better with time. But the problem continued for over a month, even with rest.

There can be other things more long lasting and even permanent that can cause a horse to be a bit lame. This is what I was concerned about.

I told my student I thought the horse might have a problem and it might not be good to buy it. Lori, my old instructor, suggested that I tell my student to consider asking a veterinarian, just to be sure. Meanwhile, the trainer was getting aggressive, insisting she didn't need that. He wanted her to hurry and close the sale. He was angry with me for suggesting she get another opinion.

The trainer and I had a showdown one day at the barn. It was a tense time. He was a pretty big deal in the horse world and the stable owner was concerned that there'd be fallout from my standing up to him. Lorie was there to support me. The trainer started yelling and threatening me. He called me all kinds of things, stormed off and arranged to take his horse away.

Unbeknownst to me, my student had consulted a veterinarian who had taken x-rays. The vet relayed that, unfortunately, the horse had changes to his navicular bone and would have gotten progressively lamer. This kind of bone degeneration is considered to be progressive and happens with some horses. It is generally thought there is no cure for it, but advances in horse medicine are always being made.

There was something off about the way the trainer was trying to intimidate me and pressure my student into the sale. I think he knew the horse had a problem and was trying to pull one over on us.

People weren't the only ones who could get aggressive. There was a gray mare on lesson board in the second-to-the-end stall next to Lady, a gentle palomino the children loved. Though this particular mare was a Thoroughbred off the track, she was anything but gentle. Many ex-racehorses have sweet temperaments, but some have been mishandled.

Just walking by the stall elicited an aggressive response. She'd pin her ears back and bare her teeth. If someone stopped to look at her, she'd lunge at them, raking her teeth on the bars. Everyone thought she was mean and a bit dangerous. When you went in the stall she wouldn't attack, but she'd make threatening gestures – pinning her ears, baring her teeth, swinging her hindquarters towards you and lifting a hind leg in readiness to kick.

In the evenings, I liked to pick out the horses' hooves – a last cleaning of the day to check for stones and any problems. The gray mare was a challenge.

One evening, I went in to do her feet. She responded by pinning her ears and tossing her head, bumping into a plastic milk jug her owner had hung from the ceiling. Sometimes people wanted a distraction for their horses, so they made a toy from a plastic bottle with a handful of gravel in it. They hung it from the ceiling in the corner, about head height for the horse to play with.

When the mare accidentally touched the jug, she jumped back, tensed, bared her teeth and snapped at me. I realized right then she was more frightened than aggressive. Most likely she had been beaten at the track for her fearful behavior. She went immediately from fear to defensiveness, to the point of aggression.

I simply stood and waited for her to settle down. I didn't punish or react, and she didn't quite know what to do. After a few minutes, she gave a big sigh and I calmly approached, picked up each foot in turn and cleaned them out. After that, when I didn't beat her for being afraid, she began to trust me.

I could more easily do things with her that others couldn't. When she got sick, I was able to take her temperature without fuss, while with others she picked up a back leg and cocked it, ready to aim a kick.

We held small horse shows for our kids and students from other local stables to compete in the summers. We washed the horses and braided their manes and tails. Most horses are docile about having their manes put into braids, but I heard from one of the barn kids that the gray mare put up a fight about having hers done. She was rearing and lashing out at the people working on her. They tried to twitch her, a form of restraint using a loop of rope on a stick twisted onto her upper lip that's an extreme form of control, used only for very short periods of time. Even with this kind of restraint, they failed to get her main and tail done.

Later, the mare's owner came into the office saying the horse was a witch. She asked me to try and braid her horse's mane. "Maybe you'll have better luck." I suspect she thought I'd fail, too.

I waited until late in the evening when everyone had left. I didn't want any distractions from people or excited kids running in and out. I wanted her to be calm and not suddenly surprised, as that seemed to set her off. Reds and Ellie, two of the teenage barn workers, stayed to help. They had been at the barn the longest and knew the horses best.

I worked slowly and took my time. Instead of tying her up, I had the girls hold her. I began with just standing on a hay bale so I could reach her mane easily. When she was calm with that, we gave her a little reward of grain.

Most everyone braids the mane from the horse's ears down to their back. I wanted to do the complete opposite of what had been attempted with her earlier in the day. I began at her withers. Whenever she tensed up, I'd stop and give her some time to process. She needed the space to find out that neither I, Reds or Ellie were going to hurt her. As soon as she relaxed, we rewarded her and continued. I went slowly, wanting to keep her from the reactive instinct of fight or flight. The more I worked, the calmer she got. Little by little, I put in the braids. It took a little longer, but we eventually got her mane and even her tail braided.

In the morning, her owner couldn't believe it. She moved her horse to another stable a few weeks later, and I've always hoped the mare ended up around people who understood she was afraid and not mean. Many of the problems she had stemmed from her fearful reactions. Someone in her past had unjustly punished her for her fear, and from that she learned to get defensive. Now, she had a habit of getting defensive and potentially aggressive whenever she was afraid.

*World in a Shoe*

*Chapter 21*

# She Really Did Want to Canter

One of my many jobs at the stable was to organize schooling shows for our pupils and those of neighboring farms. They were small, amateur affairs that let the students get a feel for competition.

Students learned the basics, from bathing and braiding their horses to the check-in process and riding with awareness in the warm-up area. They learned how to memorize a jump course and how to best maneuver around the course. They learned things like how to be considerate of other riders, even those from other stables who were our guests.

I had one student, a young girl about ten years old, who was frightened of cantering. Her mother had brought her to our stables from another, where she had been put on a horse that was too much for her level of experience. The horse ended up running away with her. It can be terrifying to be on a horse running out of control, especially when you are just learning.

I put her on the quietest horses we had and only at a walk and trot. Thanks to all I'd learned at Morven Park and Porlock Vale, I had plenty of things for her to do at these slower gaits. I set up cones for her to weave through and mini-courses of ground poles to walk over. I gave her lots of changes of direction and transition work between walk and trot. I also worked on strengthening her balance and seat. I decided to let her tell me when she was ready to try cantering again. A couple of times I asked, to which she responded no, she didn't want to try.

In the schooling shows, there were walk-trot classes for beginner riders. I thought one of these classes would be good for this student. Both she and her mom agreed.

About the same time, a pony was sent to the barn for a couple of months for exposure to different riders. It was a really nice, small bay pony that was kind and gentle. I thought she would be a great match for my pupil for the walk-trot class. All of our horses did double and triple duty the day of the show – beginner riders rode them in the easy classes and the more advanced riders took them around courses of fences. The horses worked all day long.

Every show has a designated area for riders to warm-up their mounts. They are places of controlled chaos – riders on horses and ponies going in different directions at all gaits of walk, trot and canter. Some trainers stand in the middle calling instructions, while others shout to be heard from the sidelines. The warm-up area for schooling shows was less intense than for regular shows, but riders still had to pay attention to avoid a collision. I told my students to stay to the outer edges of the warm-up area where there was less chaos.

I put my timid student on the little bay pony and told her to just walk and trot as she felt comfortable. She was doing really well, paying attention and staying out of the main areas of action. Many of my students were riding in the show, so I turned to help others get ready for their classes.

The girl's mother came over and said how happy she was that I'd helped her daughter get over her fear of cantering and that she was doing so well.

*Oh no*, I thought. I knew her daughter hadn't felt ready to try the faster gait in lessons. I was concerned the pony had been excited by the other horses and broken into a canter by itself.

I searched through the milling horses and saw my student go cantering by with a big smile on her face. I flagged her down. When she pulled up, I asked if she was alright. Flushed but with a big grin, she told me she realized she really did want to canter – so she went ahead and did it on her own. She wanted to know if it was okay to keep trying the canter. I told her it was fine as long as she kept a lookout where she was going. I watched for a bit and saw that she had a good seat, was in sync with the pony and handling her really well. I knew she wouldn't overdo it and her class was in a few minutes. It was a happy surprise for me.

The combination of giving her space and not pushing the issue with her, developing her balance and control through slower work, and pairing her with a pony she felt safe on provided her with the confidence to try cantering on her own.

I learned from my students as well as taught them. I also learned from the horses. I had to adjust to their personalities and sensitivities to teach them what I needed them to do.

One little white mare named Tasha came to us for some retraining. She was very sweet on the ground, but as soon as you put your foot in the stirrup to get on, she took off. Somewhere along the way, she'd gotten the idea she was supposed to start trotting as soon as you had one foot off the ground. The only way to get on safely was to have someone on the ground hold her head.

Most horses stay still when you get on until you tell them to go. It is especially important for lesson horses to stand quietly while students make all the needed adjustments to their equipment.

I checked that her back wasn't sore or that she had a "cold back" – these can be factors in a horse moving off quickly when mounted. She didn't seem to be frightened or an overly forward horse. It was more that she'd learned to do this.

I decided to try to teach her to stay like a dog. I used one command to stay and a different command to move off. To indicate standing in place, I applied a slight touch on the reins and a verbal command, practicing this first without trying to get on her back. I wanted her to get the idea of staying in place without the distraction of a rider.

I began by giving the command and gesture, then took a few steps away. At first she tried to follow, but I put her back where she was and renewed the command. When she didn't move, I rewarded her. She caught on pretty quickly and got so good at standing that I could go out of her sight into the barn. I gradually extended the time to about five minutes. Knowing horses, though, I did watch her through the window to make sure she didn't get distracted and wander off – which she never did.

When she had learned to stand without a rider, I transitioned to having someone get on her back. The first time or two, she began to move. So I put her back in place and gave her the command to stand. By the third time, she figured it out and stood quietly while the rider mounted and adjusted their stirrups.

We used the stand command with her from there on out, and even kids could get on by themselves without anyone holding her head.

As a teacher, I had to stay aware of each horse's little character quirks. General, a reliable bay gelding, was a horse I could put the most inexperienced rider on and trust him. Then we had a new horse come into the barn. Stonewall (or Stoney, as we called him) was a tall, rangy gray horse. Stonewall was equally pleasant and safe to ride, but General took an intense dislike to him. If they were in the same lesson together, General flew at Stoney, trying to bite him. We never turned them out in the same pasture together, nor were their stalls near one another.

It was baffling. General accepted every other horse in the barn, new ones and old friends. I could only put them in the same lesson together if I had experienced riders on each horse and they stayed well away from each other.

Maggie, an Appaloosa, could be counted on to grab a mouthful of grass with inexperienced riders, practically pulling them over her head in the process. When I put new students on her, I prepared them by showing how to keep a firm seat and have their hands remain in touch with her mouth. Maggie might test a new rider, but once she found out she couldn't catch them off guard, she gave up trying.

Lady was a very sweet palomino. It seemed as if she took special care of the riders on her back. If a student started to lose their balance, Lady stopped and waited for them to get settled before going on. She always did what was asked of her without fuss or resistance, and I don't think I ever saw her startle or shy in surprise.

While I enjoyed teaching, I was getting bored standing in the ring hour after hour telling students, "Up, down, up, down. More left rein, now kick, kick, kick – make him go." It was pretty much the same thing, day after day.

I was looking for something more. Our veterinarian knew of a position available with a woman who was just getting her barn started. She was retraining horses off the track.

I decided to go for the interview. I liked the woman and the job description, so I turned in my notice for my last few weeks of work and helped find a teaching replacement.

*World in a Shoe*

*Chapter 22*

# Lee

"You're Nicole?"

"Yes."

"Hi. I'm Lee," said the woman with short blond hair striding toward me in a pastel polo shirt, chinos and L.L. Bean boots.

I shook her hand and we walked into the barn, past hanging baskets of blooming pink and purple fuchsia. The position for which I was interviewing involved working with, caring for and exercising horses. After months of teaching riding, I knew I wasn't cut out for standing hours in the hot sun, helping people learn how to steer and stop.

Sitting in the tack room, Lee asked about my experience with horses. I'd ridden and worked with show horses, attended two riding schools for short courses, and most recently had been the manager and head instructor of a private stable.

She and her husband, Neil, recently had returned from Australia. Although Lee had an extensive background in horses, this was a new business and they were just getting started. The horses they had at the moment were "off the track," meaning ex-racehorses being retrained for jumping, showing and other forms of horse sports.

Many racehorses spend their entire lives at the track. Some get retired from racing while they have many useful years of life still in them, but they need to relearn certain basics. Racehorses are trained to run, especially when in the company of other horses. To counter this, they received retraining in patience – starting, stopping and turning while being precisely attentive to the rider.

The property was spacious with a large main house, barn, outbuildings and smaller cottages dotting the landscape overlooking the Brandywine River. Lee rented the barn and the small house nearest to it. The barn, soaring over five stories at its peak, was tidy and neatly swept. Built into a hillside, it had stalls for horses on the lower level and a hayloft above. Lee said the Amish had built it. The outer stonework of mixed tan and dark gray fieldstone was beautifully set. The stalls below were solidly constructed – the walls painted a light cream color to bring brightness inside.

Walking out of the tack room, Lee said, "Let me show you around. Right now we have about seven horses and a couple of boarders, but we are expecting more horses to come in over the summer."

Cats meandered in the shade of the aisle, looking inquisitive as we passed. A scrabbling on the pavement sounded behind us. I turned to see what the noise was.

"There they are!" she said. "Those little corgis!"

Three smiling canine faces scampered towards us, ears flopping as they bounded. Each tried to pass the others on their short legs to be first to greet us.

Bending to rub their backs, Lee pointed to a brown brindle. "This is Siegfried. The dark one is Eager Wigger, who's the mother of the little tan one, Pumpkin Pie." Eager and Pumpkin play-wrestled at our feet. "These are just the best dogs - always so happy, just a joy to have around." Their tight, compact bodies wiggled with delight as I patted their soft heads. The three nuzzled and licked my hands, their mouths in big, happy grins.

Lee said to them with obvious affection, "You all behave yourselves." Turning to me with humor she added, "Sometimes they are just little terrors." They all had white chests, white feet, and wagging tails sporting white tips.

"I didn't think corgis had tails," I said.

"Those are Pembroke corgis. These are Cardigans and they have tails," Lee explained. "The breed was originally used for herding, so we're careful not to let them out into the pastures or they try to herd the horses, who don't really pay much attention to them. But we don't want the dogs getting kicked."

"You behave, you little maniacs," she repeated to the threesome. Their intelligent eyes above grinning mouths gave the impression all they wanted to do was have fun. The dogs and cats followed us around as Lee led the way. Occasionally, the dogs mouthed one of the cats in play - the cats just shook it off. They didn't seem to mind at all.

Lee told me a bit about some of the horses. A dark brown one named Roo Boo had been trained to be ridden sidesaddle. I was surprised and said so. Sidesaddle was considered a specialty in riding.

"I learned years ago," Lee replied. Gesturing to Roo Boo she laughed and said, "He's very quiet. He likes to do nothing and rest afterward." She later showed Roo Boo at the Madison Square Garden Horse Show in New York in the sidesaddle class. It is one of the top shows in the country.

A tall bay horse tossed his head when he saw us approach. "This is Moose," Lee said. "We call him Moose because of his size. You wouldn't know it, but he is a Thoroughbred. He is owned by one of our boarders and I ride him in point-to-points." Point-to-points are races run over fences in the countryside - more casual and without the formality of the racetrack.

I discovered Lee was a versatile horsewoman. She rode in shows astride and sidesaddle. She trained and raced horses in point-to-points, and she was also a farrier – shoeing her own horses.

"Mooso, Mooso, you like to race don't you?" Lee patted his sleek neck. He'd had an operation on his larynx to help him breathe better, so his whinnies were "breathy," usually ending in a little cough. Moose was so long-legged he could practically step over pasture fences – and sometimes did to visit with horses in the other fields. He had a regal stance - head up, looking into the distance as if he were being admired for a portrait.

Lee pointed out two horses in a pasture, "The chestnut horse is Leegent and the bay, Moe, is his half-brother."

Chestnut horses have a reddish-brown coat with the same color mane and tail. Bays are brown with black manes and tails, and brown horses are dark, nearly black in color, but not a true black.

"Leegent and Moe both have the same sire and are off the track," she continued, going on to explain Moe could jump like a kangaroo. They were hoping he could be a show horse.

We agreed on terms, a couple of weeks later, in early summer, I began on trial for the job.

On my first day, we rode a circuit through trails and fields, Lee pointing out the different neighboring farms. We meandered down along the Brandywine River where a wide path had been cut and maintained. One of the neighboring farm owners enjoyed driving carriages along the river in the warm summer months. The river flooded during the winter, depositing debris – mostly dead branches and limbs - onto the path, and every spring the route was cleared for the carriages.

Sometimes during the winter months, Lee suggested we ride along the river. She'd lead Neil and me on gallops where the horses bounded over whatever happened to be blocking the muddy avenue. One year, we flew over an old, waterlogged loveseat crumpled under bare tree limbs. I was always a little unnerved by this; anything could have been on the far side to trip the horses as we landed.

In the beginning, I drove to work from where I was living, but eventually moved into an apartment on the premises. I'd arrive early in the morning as Lee was feeding the horses. When they were done eating, I'd turn them out in the paddocks and pastures, and get to work mucking the stalls while Lee did business in the office.

The barn was beautiful, with many small details that made it a joy to work in. Grates and a drainage system made it possible to wash the floors after sweeping. A trap door in the ceiling allowed hay and straw to be dropped down from the loft above. From the days when the back part of the structure housed cows, an old ventilation system drew hot air up and out, cooling the barn in hot weather. A long, wooden rail for hanging horse blankets was hinged to fold flat against the wall so it wouldn't catch a horse walking by. Three large, foaling stalls had south-facing, double Dutch doors that let in warm sunlight on cool spring days. Behind them ran an enclosed passageway with small windows where foaling could be watched without disturbing the mares.

Lee had added to the ambiance with potted plants, flowers, and paintings hung where there was wall space. She tacked cards with quotes by various philosophers on each horse's stall. This was unusual. Most barns were left largely unadorned – just the plain wood of the walls with maybe a rosette from a show.

The tack room had a heater for the winter, a fridge and a sink with hot and cold water. It was heaven to not be cleaning the leather equipment with icy water, especially when the weather turned cool. Big windows let in bright sunlight above a spacious counter Lee kept full of fruiting plants and flowers. Framed photos of horses jumping fences, competing or running in races adorned the counter and walls, along with rows of ribbons won at shows. Pink petunias outside the windows added their color to the tack room.

In the loft of the barn, gentle coos of pigeons echoed from the rafters and swallows darted in and out of the cavernous space. Bales of fragrant alfalfa, clover and timothy hay, along with golden bales of straw were stacked nearly to the roof. There's nothing like the hay-full smell of a barn loft in summer, sweet and green.

Twice a year, tractor-trailers loaded with tons of hay and straw backed up the gravel ramp. Wearing gloves, we'd heave and throw the bales, building the levels up from the heavy plank floor. Sometimes a glove would get caught in the twine and go soaring off with the bale, the person above tossing the glove back down.

The bales were stacked in levels, leaving an easy way to climb to the top. The uppermost levels were used first, then those below. The unwise pulled bales from the bottom or middle. Done often enough, the stack could become unstable and topple, bringing down tons of weight.

I rode when the stalls and barn were clean and the buckets scrubbed and refilled. Sometimes Lee and I rode together through the woods. Other times, she gave me specific things to work on with a horse. A fenced enclosure out back had jumps for schooling the horses. It was here where Lee gave me a sidesaddle lesson. With both of my legs on the same side of the horse it felt like learning to ride all over again.

I worked with some of the horses going over ground poles and low jumps. They seemed to enjoy learning. I was helping to retrain their minds; not to flex, spring and run, but to relax and respond. All of life was not a race now.

When the horses weren't being schooled in the ring, we'd ride through the surrounding countryside. The dogs would hear the horses as we came up the drive and run, barking excitedly, to meet us. Sometimes they went out with us at the beginning of a ride, but soon turned back, not able to keep up on their short legs.

Roo Boo was as pokey as Lee had indicated. I had to work to get him to go. Moose, with his longs legs, was like sitting on a rocking chair in slow motion. He was very comfortable to ride and unflappable. The only time I saw Moose flustered was when I rode him wearing a rain poncho. It billowed in the wind, so when he caught sight of it from the corner of his eye, he spooked.

Later in the summer, we took Leegent and a couple of other horses to a small show. I brought Leegent out of the van and he stood calmly watching all the activity. He was relaxed until the horses in the small ring began to canter, then his head went up and neck tensed. It appeared as if his eyes bugged out, and he began to utter small, soft groans. I can only imagine he thought it was a race unlike anything he'd ever seen before.

Moe was happy-go-lucky, yet reserved. He had a bad trick, though, of dropping his shoulder and tossing his rider, especially at a gallop. Lee said he had even done this with jockeys warming up for races.

Moe got me off one snowy day in the front field. I dusted myself off and got back on. This time, Moe grabbed the bit in his teeth and took off running down the icy hill. Generally, when a horse runs away with you, you pull them in a circle to slow and stop. But with the slippery footing, I didn't dare try and he wasn't listening to directions with the reins anyway.

Moe headed straight for the fence line – a wooden, three-rail barricade with barbed wire. I knew he could jump it easily. I'd seen him leap over higher obstacles from nearly a standstill. We hurtled down the hill toward the fence. At the last moment, he spun like a cow pony and dumped me into the barbed wire. I wasn't cut thanks to my brand-new down jacket that was now a flurry of feathers in the winter air. The snow on the ground also helped break my fall.

Neil had noticed Moe running loose and came out to find me in the snow bank with feathers drifting down. He helped me back to the barn. I was a bit banged up, but recovered fine. These kinds of things happen when you work with horses. They are forces of nature and unpredictable.

*World in a Shoe*

*Chapter 23*

# Cahoon Nights

I settled into my new job working for Lee. The animals always wanted to be around people. On some farms, the dogs are unfriendly and the cats skittish, slinking off to hide in the dark places of the hayloft. Not here. No matter where you stopped or sat, whether in a chair or on the curve of lawn by the drive, a dog or cat would meander over, jump up, look you in the face and settle in. Sometimes to play, sometimes just to be.

Everywhere I went, El Tigra, the brown tabby, followed on my heels. It felt like he was trying to convert me to a cat person. Growing up, we'd pretty much only had dogs. I thought cats were nice enough – good to have around the barn to catch mice and rats. El Tigra was under my feet so much that one day I plopped him in an empty wheelbarrow. He stayed in it for the whole ride, and only got out when I parked the barrow and walked away.

His aeronautics first surprised me when I was mucking a stall. Bent over, spreading straw with a pitchfork, I felt something land on my back with a thump. As quickly as I straightened up, El Tigra clambered to perch on my shoulder and stare into my face. Time and again, he'd perform this flying feat. Once on my shoulder, he'd try and stay there as long as possible. If I sat down for a moment of rest during the day, he was on my lap, presenting his ears and face for attention and scratching.

Eventually, I put El Tigra on the back of a horse wearing a blanket to see what he would do. He arched his back a bit for balance, poked his nose out as though I might pet him, and then watched the world go by as I led the horse around. Nothing seemed to faze El Tigra. He occasionally took the shortest route to his destination with no regard for his safety, darting between a moving horse's legs while Lee commented, "That cat must have a death wish or something."

After I'd moved to the farm, El Tigra sometimes followed me to my apartment, slept in my room and came back with me the next morning. His orange brother, Lawrence, was a bit more reserved around people.

One morning, I found Lawrence dead. He'd gotten into one of the bins in the barn and had died in the night. I buried him in the woods behind the jumping ring and then spent some time sitting in the tack room. El Tigra, ever present in my lap, looked intently into my face. He gently reached out a paw, touched one of my tears and brought it to his mouth, then went back to looking in my eyes.

A week or two later, someone brought us a pure white kitten they found on the side of the road. Lee named him Max. Kodak and Easter, an orange tabby and a calico, arrived the following spring, a gift from one of the boarders.

\* \* \* \*

"Not again!" I thought.

I shrugged my body in exasperation as I heard scrabbling on the wood floor in the dark, then silence. Why did I think it would be fun to spend the night with the baby raccoons in the room? I had to be at the barn earlier than usual the next day – Lee had a horse running at the track. Although most of the horses were there for retraining, she had some that were still racing.

This was before I'd moved to the farm, and Lee suggested I spend the night in the extra room upstairs rather than make the early commute.

Along with horses, barn cats and corgi dogs, Lee took in stray raccoons. She had a soft spot for babies who somehow became separated from their siblings and mother. Sometimes she'd find them on the path while riding through the woods. After ascertaining the little orphan was healthy and not sick, Lee tucked it in her shirt and brought it home.

She fed and raised them, and when old enough, they'd go back into the woods. Somewhere after raccoon adolescence, they want more and more independence. They'd sleep on the screened porch during the day and foray into the trees around the house at night. Eventually, they spent all their time away from the porch, disappearing to live in the wild.

While they were small, they stayed in the house or in a large cage in the barn. They got lots of attention, and Lee gave them all names that ended in "cahoon" – Wacky-cahoon, Minna-cahoon, Wally-cahoon, etc. They were bold and fearless, regularly wrestling with the dogs and aggressively pouncing on the cats. They were scrappy and knew their own minds.

Lying on the cot in the guest room, I heard a tick, tick, tick. Hesitant, little tapping claws crossed the floor in my direction. Soon, miniature hands began an inquisitive search over my legs and up my body.

Even a kitten eventually gets tired of jumping on your feet under the blanket and goes to sleep. Not the raccoons. They play and play and play - all through the night. Raccoons are nocturnal, up at night and asleep during the day. Not only do they pounce on you and each other, they pry into everything. When they weren't jumping on me, they rustled and rummaged through my gear on the table. Whatever thudded to the floor, I eventually left there.

The cahoons, as we came to call them, got into everything. No one's personal effects were left unscathed. They figured out snaps, zippers and buttoned-down flaps. Whatever they could put their hands on they claimed for their own – if it was something shiny, even better. They went after jewelry, compacts, lipsticks, pens, pencils, hairbrushes, crumpled foil and bones from the trash, paper clips, eyeglasses from the table, and change from the bottom of handbags. They were the cutest little kleptomaniacs you could ever imagine.

One day, Lee cleaned the sofa slipcovers and found the raccoons had carved out a cache site for their trinkets. She later told me she found a watch, change, dog kibble and the bones from a roasted chicken. She even found a pen she'd been looking all over for.

Along with snaps and zippers, they figured out how to get doors open, including the refrigerator. Food ended up all around the house. Lee tried to get them trained to a litter box, but they just hopped out and used the floor wherever they pleased.

Anything a raccoon picks up to eat gets washed in water. An old-fashioned white, enameled dish tub in the kitchen served as the dog's water bowl. It was low enough for the dogs to drink out of, yet had a broad lip so it wouldn't tip over. It was fun to watch the raccoons with pieces of apple and other food. They dunked the tidbit in the water and began to quickly rotate it between their paws. After a few minutes, dripping up to their elbows, they'd pull it out and beat a hasty retreat with their prize.

Occasionally, Lee gave them ice cubes. They'd toddle quickly to the water dish and began washing. As the ice got smaller the raccoons grew more agitated. Finally, when the ice had melted, they launched a frantic search, practically swimming in the dish up to their chins. They were only given ice a few times. It was funny, but also a bit heartbreaking to watch them search in vain.

The raccoons also had a dark side to them. Two tiny kittens were dropped at the farm – people seem to think horse barns are a good place to bring abandoned kittens. Of course, we took them in. We accepted whatever was brought to us, even the baby rabbit found on the road late at night. They got veterinary care, worming, annual shots, and were spayed and neutered.

The two new kittens must have been just past six weeks - too young to be free in the barn where they might get stepped on by a horse. The first night, Lee locked them in a cage inside the tack room.

We thought they'd be safe with the adolescent raccoons also in the tack room, but free to roam about.

In the morning, the cage was empty. All that was left was an ear and small piece of leg. The raccoons had made a meal of the kittens.

*World in a Shoe*

## Chapter 24

# Philbee

By the middle of the night, it was no longer fun to be explored by inquisitive little raccoon hands touching my face and body. Everyone was asleep, and I couldn't move the pair to the cage in the barn without making too much noise. They succeeded in keeping me up all night, and as the sun cracked the horizon, Minna and Wally were slumped in a corner together.

Staggering out of bed, I eyed the two of them sleeping peacefully with mixed feelings of annoyance and affection. The last thing I needed was to be tired on the day I had my first experience at a racetrack.

I slipped into my clothes and walked down to the barn. Lee was already up doling out the morning feed.

Walking quickly with buckets she said, "Turn out the boarder horses as soon as they are done eating and get all the stalls done early."

"Right," I said, gathering the wheelbarrow, rake and pitchfork.

"Is John Randall up yet?" Lee asked as I passed by carrying water buckets to scrub in the yard. John Randall, her adolescent nephew, was visiting for a few days and staying in the other guest room.

"His door was still shut when I came down the stairs," I replied.

"That nephew of mine is going to sleep his whole life away. He comes for a visit and all he wants to do is stay in bed."

"Do you want me to go and get him up?" I asked.

"No, keep working here. There's a lot to do before we leave. If he's still asleep when Neil gets back from gassing up the car, I'll have Neil wake him," she said as she headed for the tack room.

I walked the horses out to their pastures and set to work on the stalls. Philbee, the horse who was running in the race, stayed in and watched his buddies out in the field. Always very good-natured, he didn't seem to mind being kept inside.

Philbee had arrived at the farm shortly after I started work. He was a sweet, brown horse with a kind and easy-going temperament. Sometimes when turned out in the pasture, he'd stay by the gate and watch our morning activities. At times it seemed he preferred the company of people to that of the other horses. I refilled his water bucket, gave his dark glossy neck a pat, and then turned to sweeping the aisle.

Lee flew out of the tack room. "John Randall's set the house on fire!" She took off running to the house. I ran after her to see what I could do to help.

It was the kitchen. John Randall had been cooking bacon and the grease caught on fire. When he threw the pan in the sink, the curtains above caught on fire. Luckily, the fire died out after that, but the flames had scorched the walls and left the curtains in shriveled, black tatters. He phoned down to the barn in a panic.

After all the uproar, we headed back to the barn. Lee and I bustled around, finishing the morning's chores. As we passed each other in the aisle, Lee called out things she wanted me to do or listed items she wanted me to pack.

"Is the ring bit on Philbee's bridle? Don't forget the blinkers, the blue and green ones. They are hanging on the hook beneath his bridle. Do you have the brushes packed?" Lee asked as she whizzed by me with papers in her hand. "Put poultice in the trunk. It's in the cupboard under the counter."

"I put the ring bit on yesterday, the brushes are packed, and I put cotton flannel, bandages and liniment in as well," I called after her.

"Great."

Lee spied her husband returning from getting gas in the car. "Neil! Where have you been? Have you hitched the car to the trailer? John Randall set the kitchen on fire! Teenagers, they just don't think. We have to hurry or we're going to be late. Can you put hay in Philbee's hay net? Is the map in the car?"

"Yes, the car is hitched and I have the map. Lee, settle down, there's time," he said.

Neil looked in the trunk I was filling with equipment. "Do you think you have everything we'll need?"

"I hope so," I said. "I've only been to horse shows, never to the track."

"Not now, you crazy little dogs," Lee said, weaving through the corgis who were play-wrestling around her feet.

"Nicole," she called, "throw in a handful of screw eyes and an extra hoof pick, and don't forget a bucket for drinking water for Philbee." She headed for the barn entrance as her nephew arrived. "John Randall, it's about time you showed up. Here, put these things in the car. No, the backseat." Turning around, she asked, "Are the raccoons in the cage? Neil! The dogs have to be shut in the house before we go!"

"I know, Lee! Take it easy, would you? Everything is fine." Neil looked at me and shook his head.

She trotted past without losing rhythm or focus. "I just have to get some forms in the house before we go." She called over her shoulder, "Is an extra halter and lead shank packed? Anyone who needs to use the bathroom, better use it now. Eager, Siegfried, Pumpkin! Come on doggies! Everybody in the house!"

Lee had enough energy for all of us, and my tiredness from lack of sleep was forgotten in the adrenalin rush of getting ready to go.

Philbee, always the picture of tranquil poise, walked onto the trailer calm and happy. Neil, John Randall and I, with Lee driving, headed out on the Pennsylvania interstate. Our destination: Penn National Racetrack.

After an hour and a half on freeways, we took an exit that wound around to the rear entrance of the track. Lee pulled up in front of the guard booth.

Due to the sums of money involved, racing is strictly regulated. The entire stabling area of each track, known as the backstretch, is fenced in with a guarded gate. This ensures that only the horses who are supposed to be there are. Every horse that enters and leaves is checked and their papers examined. Horses were identified by a tattoo on the inside of their upper lip. After a Thoroughbred is born, registered and named, he must be given a tattoo before he can run on the track.

The security was such that in order to get a job at the track, you were fingerprinted and checked for a criminal record. Even people who only mucked stalls and walked the hot horses had to have their record checked with the authorities.

Lee got out to handle the paperwork. She had her trainer's license, which was all she needed to enter. For single visits of one night, the rest of us were given special badges we clipped to our shirts.

She got directions to the visitor's barn, the temporary stabling for horses brought to the track for just one race. We drove by identical, unpainted wood and cinder block structures housing forty or more horses each. The only difference in each building was the large, stenciled numbers and letters on the sides. With rows and rows of sameness, it looked like a treeless, grassless, industrial complex.

Arriving at the right letter and number, we unloaded Philbee. Neil walked him around to stretch his legs. I helped Lee unload the equipment and get the stall ready.

"Nicole, stay with Philbee. Neil, John Randall and I are going to the office to check in," Lee said.

"Okay," I replied, gathering up brushes.

"We're picking up something for dinner. You want a hot dog and soda?" she asked.

"That would be great."

Lee unhitched the old blue station wagon from the trailer and they headed to the track office near the grandstand. I checked on Philbee, gave his already shining, dark coat another brush and made sure his hooves were clean.

## World in a Shoe

My excitement was building. I saw people walking in and out of nearby barns with buckets and supplies. I was curious, but didn't dare go more than ten steps from Philbee's stall.

Some tracks hold daytime races and some run at night. Penn National had nighttime racing, but it was policy that all horses running had to be on the premises before the start of the program. Racing began around 7:30 p.m., with the starting gate ringing open approximately every half hour through the last race, which was around midnight. Philbee was in one of the later races, so we had hours to wait.

I sat on the trunk by the door. Other trainers arrived with their horses and found their assigned stalls. It was fascinating to see the different way grooms handled the same small procedures. Clearly apparent was the bond each felt with his charge. I heard them murmuring to their horses. Every animal had different needs in handling pre-race stress. Some horses were walked continuously around the shed row, while others stayed tied in their stalls away from distractions.

From down the barn I heard a disembodied voice. "Settle down. Don't run your race before you get on the track."

A thin old man in rumpled jeans went by leading a chestnut horse. It tossed its teak-colored head and started to prance. He stroked the silken neck. "Now, now, don't go getting fussy and nervous, you'll do fine." The horse relaxed into a rhythmic walk beside him.

Philbee placidly watched the goings on, occasionally poking his soft brown nose in my direction to see if I had a carrot or other treat. He'd had a meal early that morning but little else. He needed to be lean with nothing weighing him down for the race.

The loudspeakers in the barn crackled and announced, "All horses for the first race, head to the paddock." It was the groom's job to lead the horse to the saddling area over by the grandstand. Horses passed by in varying states of tension and excitement. Some were relaxed, while others were sweating and jogging in place, eager to go. I caught snatches of words from their grooms:

"You're gonna do it this time. I know you can."

"Don't fight the jockey. Just listen and run when it's time."

"Bring home the check, old man."

From the barn on the backside, you don't hear the track announcer naming the horses as they come from the saddling area or the call of the race as they dash from the gate. What you do hear is the roar. The crowd in the grandstand comes alive as the horses run down the homestretch to the finish. Across the one-mile track, I heard the roar.

Philbee heard it, too. He stood rooted, head high, nostrils flared and ears pricked forward. He circled the stall three times, stopping at the door on each turn, quivering, listening intently.

"We got you a Coke, is that okay?" Lee asked, coming down the aisle.

She went in with Philbee. "How's my Philbert? Are you all excited about racing?" I heard her patting his neck. "How has he been?" she asked.

"He's fine, but he really livened up when the crowd started yelling," I replied through bites.

Horses returning from their races were bathed and their grooms began the slow process of hot walking – cooling down the horses by making circuits around the barn.

Lee explained if Philbee won that night, we'd go to the "spit barn" instead of coming right back to the visitor's barn. All the top finishers of each race went to a small stable to be tested for illegal drugs. It was called the spit barn because when testing first began, officials checked the horse's saliva. Now, though they collected urine, the name had stuck and spit barn is still used.

There is an interesting mentality on the track and a jargon that goes with it. If Lee asked a passing groom how their horse did, they answered, "He beat two," or "He beat three." Even if the horse came second-to-last, they said, "He beat one." Lee counseled me to always answer that way if I was ever asked.

Finally, they called Philbee's race over the loudspeakers. Lee put the bridle, halter and lead on him. Sometimes a fit horse can get fractious on the way to the paddock, so Neil led Philbee over. Philbee was a perfect gentleman, as always.

A pony is used when a horse is really a handful. Not to be confused with small-sized ponies that children ride, the term ponying is used when someone leads the racehorse from the back of a full-sized, quiet horse. Most of the time, the stability of a calm animal is enough to settle a keyed-up Thoroughbred. Ponying is also used sometimes during morning exercising.

The track was much bigger than it looked from the grandstand, and the sandy surface softer and deeper than I'd imagined. It was a workout to walk the half-mile or so to the grandstand, and it wasn't a slow pace, either.

The saddling went smoothly and the jockey, wearing Lee's bright blue and green silks, was lifted onto Philbee's back. Out they went to the track, Philbee trotting a little in anticipation. There was a moment of stillness as the horses went into the gate. The ringing of the bell floated across the infield as the gate popped open and a surge of horses flowed down the backstretch.

Philbee finished somewhere in the middle. Even after the race, he had plenty of pep and wanted to go some more. We washed him down back at the barn, placed a light blanket called a cooler on him, and took turns hot walking him around the shed row.

The race itself lasted only a little over a minute. The hot walking, grooming and bandaging of Philbee's legs took up most of the time. We loaded him on the trailer after midnight, gave him a net of hay and headed back to the farm.

It was nearly 2:30 in the morning when we pulled in the drive – that hushed time of night when even crickets are quiet. Lee put Philbee in his stall. I checked on the other horses and made sure they had water for the night. Then we all headed up to the house and I fell into a deep slumber on the cot in the guestroom, this time without the raccoons. In three hours, Lee and I had to be up and put in another full day's work at the barn.

*World in a Shoe*

*Chapter 25*

# Jokes and Vacation

It was hard work, but I enjoyed it. Lee trusted my judgment with the horses, and they were all making progress.

I found out both she and Neil had quite a sense of humor. For birthdays, Lee arranged scavenger hunts with clues written on little slips of paper hidden in nooks and crannies around the barn and pastures. One year, I made a follow-the-string maze up and down the aisle and through the stalls for Lee on her birthday.

She and Neil took turns surprising each other with their annual vacations. The year I started work, Lee had made arrangements for a trip to the Caribbean. Swearing me to secrecy, she made me promise to tell Neil when he asked – and she was sure he'd try - that she was taking him to the Potato Festival in Idaho.

He did ask, and after a lot of reluctance I told him he was going to Idaho. He didn't look pleased, but I think he bought it, because it was the kind of thing Lee might actually do. I suspect poor Neil still thought they were going to Idaho up to the moment they got to the ticket counter. They had a great vacation.

We played jokes on each other, which was a lot of fun. There was a rubber snake that had a longevity beyond the other tricks. I don't remember exactly how it came to be in the barn. We kept hiding it back and forth. Lee would coil it in the box of horse brushes or I'd slip it on top of the sack of grain in the feed bin. That snake circulated all over the barn, in and out of drawers and cupboards. We even got Neil a few times with it.

Along with being an all-around horsewoman, Lee was an accomplished artist and Neil a potter. One of the storage rooms in the barn was set up as his studio, with a wheel for throwing the clay pots. They displayed their works of art around their house, and people got to see them when they held parties.

Lee and Neil threw great parties. I decided to go as a cat for their Halloween costume party. I'd planned to glue yarn all over a sweatshirt but ran out of time. So I bandaged up the unfinished parts, grabbed a crutch and sling, and went as a cat-astrophe.

We put in long hours every day, often not finishing until after dark. Lee was a blacksmith and taught me a little about shoeing a horse after she injured her shoulder. It is not easy holding up their leg and foot. Sometimes the horse gets a little lazy and leans on you. Try holding up a piano on your knee and you'll know what it feels like.

It was a good place to work. Different places have their own presence, and the farm and land were harmonious for me. I thrived there. The land and atmosphere of the place were kind: enough water, enough shade from the sun, enough shelter from storms - beauty to the eye, and access to openness and nature.

There is a calm that comes at the twilight time of day, a relaxing and letting go into peaceful stillness. When I got the chance, I loved to walk the fields in the evenings. The corgis ran and bounced along behind, stopping to wrestle with each other. The cats came on the walks, too. They kept to short gallops among the cornrows, glimpses of brown, orange, white and calico between the green stalks.

The shift from day to night was reflected in the moods of the horses as well. The keen alertness of the morning and afternoon eased. The evening brought contented sighs. As light moved to full dark, the horses paused more often, ears cocked, attentive to some far off sound. The night was for listening.

*Chapter 26*

# John Randall

John Randall, Lee's nephew, came up from Maryland to visit in the summers. Lee gave him riding lessons and taught him about taking care of horses. I can't imagine what it must have been like to have an aunt who trained racehorses for a living. He'd always stay in one of the guestrooms. He even tried one night with the raccoons in the room, after which he said he never wanted to do that again - they'd kept him up all night. I laughed and told him they did the same thing to me.

As John Randall progressed with his lessons, Lee decided it was time for him to have his own horse. She kept this a secret though, and began a hunt for a suitable mount. Since he was an adolescent, John Randall's horse would have to be very quiet and well mannered.

Lee found a bay horse retired from the track named Pooh Bear. I didn't know if that was his real racing name. Sometimes we didn't know the names they were registered under, and after they retired from racing it didn't matter.

While running at tracks, a horse's registered name must match its papers and it will have that name for its whole racing career. Sometimes, people elect not to continue using a racehorse's official name after its retirement from the track. In that case, they usually choose something more reflective of its personality.

Pooh Bear was gentle and kind. He showed no inclination to buck or run away with his rider and seemed to have one gear: plodding along at a quiet pace. He'd had a minor operation to his throat, the same kind of surgery that Moose had had, giving Pooh Bear a whispery whinny, too. Even when turned out with the other horses, he preferred to graze or amble about and not join in cantering around. He was the perfect first horse for John Randall.

Lee swore us all to secrecy in case her nephew called on the phone for some reason. On the day John Randall was to arrive, I washed Pooh Bear thoroughly and combed out his dark mane and tail. Lee came down to the barn carrying big red bows and a ribbon for me to put on him.

Lee told John Randall there was a surprise at the barn. He came down the hill and I led Pooh Bear out. John Randall was overjoyed.

Mrs. Howard, Lee's mother, was also there to see the surprise. Lee took pictures of a smiling John Randall, Mrs. Howard, me and Pooh Bear. We tacked Pooh Bear up and John Randall went for a ride. It was really fun to see him get his horse. It reminded me of when I got my first horse, a surprise from my mother.

He rode every day, and when he had to go back to Maryland, Pooh Bear stayed with us. We took care of him between John Randall's visits to the farm.

\* \* \* \*

Retraining horses continued, and occasionally Philbee ran in races at Penn National – which meant getting home late at night. I didn't really mind. It was fun at the track and I figured I could catch up on my rest the next night.

Late one evening after returning from the track, I heard the horses in the front pasture making a lot of noise. They were running about in the dark near the gate, upset. Over the fence I made out Moe's frizzy mane and forelock that had a tendency to stand up around his ears. Reaching to pet him, I felt something warm and sticky. Moe lurched away from my hand. I turned towards the light and saw blood. He had gotten injured. I brought him in to see how bad it was.

He was cut and bitten all over, and had marks from being kicked. One of the other horses in the pasture had really gone after him, but there was no way to know which horse had done it. We checked the others and they were all right, none of them cut up. We kept Moe in for the night.

Sometimes horses get in an altercation with each other and they work it out. Occasional cuts and scrapes aren't uncommon when horses are out in groups together, but not like what happened to Moe.

A few days later, another horse turned up with bites and cuts. Then one day we heard the horses running and agitated. This time, we saw Leegent chasing and biting them. We didn't know why he began doing this, going after the other horses. He had been turned out with them for years.

We moved Leegent to the orchard, a small pasture adjacent to the front field where he could be by himself. He was fine for a while. Then he broke through the fence.

At the farm alone, I heard the commotion. Leegent had singled out Pooh Bear, was hounding and chasing him. Pooh Bear couldn't outrun him and was desperately trying to avoid the raking bites.

I ran and got a whip, a long one. By the time I got down the hill, Leegent had Pooh Bear on the ground, pummeling him with his hooves. It looked like he had a single-minded purpose, to kill Pooh Bear.

I've never had to attack a horse before. I've had to calm them when afraid and encourage them when sulky. It was terrifying to stand in front of Leegent's rearing form and soundly slash with the whip, shout and intimidate him off. The rage and fear in me met whatever force was acting in him. In the end, I won out.

I hated to do it. I hated more the sound of his hooves thudding on Pooh Bear's prone body. I felt taken over, driven – as insane as he was.

I got Pooh Bear up and safely out of the pasture. He was okay, just cuts and bruises. Leegent settled down with Pooh Bear out of sight. I separated Leegent from the other horses and locked him in his stall.

We never turned out Leegent with another horse ever again. It seemed he'd gotten a lust for attacking other horses. He had a twist in his mind. We never found out why and, he was soon sent to a sale.

*World in a Shoe*

*Chapter 27*

# New Faces

During the winter, we went to a Thoroughbred sale in Maryland. Lee drove us down to see the prospects.

The sales catalogue listed the horses, age, bloodlines, race record and earnings. But the little book told you virtually nothing about the horse itself, whether it had crooked legs, strong or weak tendons and ligaments, a kind or problematic temperament. For that, you had to see the horse firsthand. I followed Lee for hours through the barns while she looked over possible purchases.

The horse may have raced recently and been placed in the sale, or months could have gone by since the last time they ran. No reasons were given. Anything was possible - they could have started having leg problems due to the strain of racing or they weren't making enough money to pay for their expenses. A horse could have fabulous bloodlines from winning families and turn out to not have any speed at all. Racing was a financially risky business. Sometimes owners went broke and had to sell their horses.

You never really knew what you were getting when you bid at a sale and brought a horse home. There was always the hope a different trainer and new regime would do the trick and make the horse a winner. If his conformation (build and bone structure) was good and he looked sound, you trusted you could handle anything else that came up about the horse.

For the most part, the horses were what they were made out to be. But sometimes we discovered there was more to them than met the eye.

That winter we had four unknowns come into our barn from the sale: an untrained youngster we dubbed Sneaky, a chestnut mare named Trip It, a bay horse called Lou Woodie, and a little imp named Cosnav.

Trip It, a chestnut mare with a white blaze on her face, had little white hairs sprinkled throughout her reddish coat. She had a calm nature. If something excited her, she'd watch intently, but not fuss and fidget like some horses who get tense and move around. She surprised us the morning after the sale by jumping a three-rail wooden fence with snow plowed up against it. I had put her in the small turnout area next to the barn while I cleaned her stall. She trotted around at a leisurely jog. I expected her to stop at the fence, but without hesitation, she leapt it and the snow bank like a gazelle, landing between the parked cars. She continued her jog down the driveway. Lee went and brought her back. She had potential for show jumping. Most horses don't jump fences by themselves without a rider.

Sneaky still had to go through training, but seemed eager to investigate everything.

Lou Woodie, a bay with no white on him at all, was a rascal. I was riding him one afternoon up a tree-lined trail toward a field when suddenly he erupted in a bucking fit. No bee sting, no blowing paper to scare him. He bucked just because he wanted to. Tipping his head and shaking it at an angle, he made small squeals as he leapt in the air. After a verbal "Lou! Stop it!" I pushed him forward with a squeeze from my legs and we continued up the trail.

Lou came from the tracks out west and hadn't raced for a while. Because he didn't come with a history, we didn't know why he'd had so much time off, whether he had gone lame or had just soured on running.

Lee entered Lou in a race the following spring and he gave us quite a surprise. He lagged almost last until the final turn. As the horses straightened into the homestretch, Lou put on a burst of speed. He came from behind, passing the others to place second at 40 to 1 odds. Lou ran all his races that way, waiting until the last possible minute to start running – heartbreak finishers they were called. You never knew if they were going to be able to have enough speed and stamina to overtake the other horses in time.

At times, Lou was impatient. A group of us were riding and had jumped from one pasture to the next. Lee was making Lou wait his turn. I cleared the fence and looked back to see Lou up on his hind legs. He slipped, lost his balance and sat, rolling over backwards onto Lee, cracking her shoulder blade. Lou was in obvious discomfort himself.

The vet arrived, looked Lou over and gently moved his tail. Lou's knees buckled a bit – he'd broken his tail when he sat down. It healed fine and he went on to run and win races.

Dark brown Cosnav was an imp. Though around three years old, he had the build of a yearling: fine boned, narrow chested, and a thin neck. He was short for a racehorse – just a few inches taller than a pony, which put his back at least four inches below that of most of the other horses in the barn. Small, tense and intense, the term bantamweight would best describe him. He had the fine hair and thin skin found on many sensitive chestnut horses. There was a kind of edginess to him, a natural excitement with the events of life going on around him.

When he whinnied, his whole body shook. He often pranced when walking, holding his head and neck arched; not pulling against the lead, but dancing in place, eager to get out to the pasture or get going for exercise. Set loose in the pasture, he'd pivot on the spot and take off running. Riding him put me in mind of a car with a stuck accelerator. If you let up on the brake, even a little bit, he would just keep getting faster and faster.

Occasionally, Cosnav would get the horses in the field riled up. He'd run past the others who were peacefully grazing and kick out at them in play. Sometimes the horses just shook their heads in angry response. Other times they'd take off running after Cosnav, who'd be leading the way with his tail up. One day, he picked on a horse that had a reputation of being a bit of a bully and outran him, too.

Cosnav didn't have any problem challenging other horses that were much bigger than him. But let the veterinarian try to give him a shot and he'd just about tear the barn down trying to get away. I got more than one bruise helping to hold him while the vet worked on him.

One afternoon, Lee entered the barn in a hurry.

"Did you see what happened to Cosnav?" She sounded excited.

"No, what?" I had just arrived back at the barn.

"Someone cut off his tail!" she exclaimed.

"What? Where?"

"Out in the pasture – they climbed over the fence!"

"They cut the bone?" I asked, shocked. A horse's tail is comprised of a bone with long hairs growing off it so he can swish flies.

"No, just the bottom of his tail," Lee said. "I think they wanted a souvenir. People will do anything."

The pastures fronted a road that sightseers used for scenic drives. Occasionally, they stopped to watch the horses. It was unbelievable that someone was brazen enough to climb the fence.

I went out to look. Sure enough, Cosnav's black tail was short. The hairs were sheared off at the end of his tailbone high above his hocks, the middle joint in his back leg.

I was a bit shocked and dismayed as I trudged back to the barn. When I got back from the pasture, Lee was laughing.

She'd played another trick on me. She had been the one to trim Cosnav's tail and had decided to make it really short. She said it had gotten straggly and thought he'd look better this way. Now, with his short tail and his mane's tendency to stand up on end, he resembled the horses from eighteenth century hunting and racing prints.

*Chapter 28*

# Nahma

Nahma came to the farm. He was dark, almost charcoal-colored with a really sweet temperament. He had raced at the track for a number of years and was very level-headed. Some racehorses have a fiery temperament to go with their speed. Even the quiet ones who are racing-fit can feel full of themselves and act up occasionally.

Horses that had been on the track most of their lives sometimes didn't know what to do out on trails. They often hadn't seen open spaces and wildlife since they were young. From an early age, most racehorses only set foot on manicured ground kept free of obstacles and debris that can injure them. When they arrived at the farm, some of the horses stumbled over roots and stones until they learned to watch the ground and be nimble on their feet.

From the start, Nahma was a dream out on trails. Before coming to us he must have had some experiences outside of the pasture. Nothing startled him, not the white-tailed deer that bounded through the trees ahead of us nor pheasants fluttering up from the tall grass by his feet. I didn't need to keep a tight rein on him; he was happy to go at whatever pace I had set.

His kind nature came to the front one winter morning. Christmas day dawned cold and overcast, with shades of yellow and orange seeping through the thin, cottony clouds. It was cold beyond frost, the grass having long ago turned brown and curled itself into icy cocoons that crunched underfoot.

When you work with horses, there is no such thing as a holiday. They need care every day of the year. In the early hours on this particular chilly morning, I donned my double thermal long john underwear and set about tending the horses. Entering the barn, the chilly air outside that held my breath suspended like a wraith gave way to the warm smell of sweet hay. The hungry horses whickered greetings. I fed and watered them, and set about cleaning the stalls.

Having completed the barn chores, I was ready for my Christmas morning. I joined Lee, Neil and some friends for brunch and presents. Along with brunch came mimosas - champagne with orange juice.

Warmed by mimosas, our lively discussion became a decision to go for a Christmas ride. The grass crackled underfoot as our laughing group made its way to the barn. We got all the horses tacked in gear, ourselves zipped and booted, and with a clatter of hooves we set off down the carriage path that goes along the Brandywine River. The naked, barren trees and ice shelves at the river's edge held a surreal kind of beauty in the stark gray of winter.

We stopped at one of the river crossing points and considered going to the other side. In summer, when the water is sparkling clear and low, wading across is no problem. But in winter with increased rain and snowmelt, the Brandywine rages. It becomes a muddy, angry torrent. Rafters and canoers often rode the swollen river in the spring, and drownings were not unheard of. If they fell in, they sometimes didn't make it out.

While we discussed if it was safe to cross, Stephanie rode Nahma into the river up to his knees. I expected her to turn back or that level-headed Nahma would balk at going in water near freezing. I don't think any of us believed they'd go any further, but they forged right in.

Suddenly the water was broadsiding Nahma, washing up over his back. The strong current swept him off his feet. He struggled desperately to keep his head above the roiling water. Stephanie lost her balance, slid off and vanished under the surface. Then Nahma, too, was completely submerged. They had both disappeared.

Galvanized, we galloped alongside the surging river, yelling and searching for any sign of them. Nahma's brown head popped out of the water for a moment before he was sucked back down. The churning current tumbled him over and over, we saw his head then feet, then head and then feet again, and then nothing but muddy rushing water. There was no sign of Stephanie anywhere.

Near the far bank, a dark shape appeared above the surface – Nahma swimming to the opposite shore. If he had tried to turn around in the river to come back he surely would have drowned.

He made it to the other side and heaved himself up the mud and rock slope. There was something tangled in his tail. It was Stephanie!

She had somehow stayed with Nahma and wrapped her arm in his long, dark tail. He pulled her to safety without kicking or knocking her loose from her grip. Waterlogged and shaky, they stood on the far bank.

Now, we had a new problem. They were wet and it was freezing cold. They were on the far bank and crossing the river again was out of the question. A train trestle and bridge spanned the river farther along, but Stephanie didn't know how to get to it.

We called across for her to stay put, quickly splitting into two groups. One was to guide her back to the farm, while the rest of us raced to the house to run a hot bath for Stephanie and prepare to take care of wet and cold Nahma.

They both looked like drowned rats as they came up the lane. Stephanie was smiling and looked a bit chagrinned. Nahma took it all in stride, as though swimming in an icy river and saving the life of his rider were all normal occurrences.

While the situation turned out well in this case, I'd never advocate drinking and riding. It is a dangerous combination and I never did it again. Working with horses requires you to be present with all of your faculties. The ability to make clear decisions about safety could save you and your horse's life.

*World in a Shoe*

*Chapter 29*

# Waves of Instinctive Action

You use all of your senses when working with horses. It is a whole body experience – sight, sound, smell, feel and taste.

Sight – when looking at the condition of their coat, and health and tone of their body.

You smell the hay to make sure it is good. You can't rely on your eyes – sometimes they aren't enough to detect the spores of mold on bad hay that could sicken or even kill the horses. Generally, hay is dried well and is safe to feed to horses and cattle. But if the hay became damp during baling or transport, mold can begin to grow.

When hay is really moldy, you can see and smell the bad section right away. The tiny mold spores can spread and grow into sections called flakes that look clean to the eye. Taking the time to smell the flake of hay, you can detect the musty, off-odor. Even a bale that looks good throughout could have a flake or two of mold. Moldy hay upsets the horse's digestive system and they can get colic or even die from it.

The odor of the manure in the morning alerts you if the horses are sick or have eaten something that doesn't suit them. Horses fed a specific, regular diet will have manure that smells pretty much the same day after day. When there is a change in diet, the manure will have a different smell. Too much grazing on young spring grass for a horse living in a stable can cause diarrhea. In addition to being runny, the manure can have a strong smell, telling you the horse had too much. Over-grazing on spring grass can cause colic and also trigger a foot ailment called laminitis, both of which can be very serious for the horse.

You know to keep an extra close eye on them to make sure they are all right.

If there is too much ammonia in the wet straw, you check to ensure they have enough clean water. If they have enough clean water, then you make note of how much they are drinking. Some horses just have more ammonia in their urine naturally. You make a mental note of those horses. The ones who don't have strong ammonia in the urine and then have a day or two when it is there need to be watched.

You taste their feed to see if it's too salty or too sweet. Some horse feeds are a mix of grains such as oats, barley and cracked corn. Different balances of minerals and roughage are added, and the mix is bound with molasses. Mostly, horses need good quality hay and grass, with grains to supplement the diet. Horses competing in sports events need more grains for energy and protein.

The sound of their rhythmic chewing tells you they are content. A short pause indicates interest in something. If you don't hear a horse chewing at feeding time, you check on them because there is something amiss. One job I worked, I noticed a horse not eating at feeding time. It turned out he had the early stages of colic.

You can tell a horse has a loose shoe by the higher pitched "tink" it makes when hitting the ground as opposed to shoes that are still tight and make a solid "clop" sound. Loose shoes need to be tightened or replaced so they don't trip the horse. You can also detect if a horse might be getting lame on a particular leg. Its step on the sore leg is shorter and lighter than on the other legs. The impact of the hoof makes a lighter, higher-pitched sound amidst the solid "clop" sound of the healthy legs. They nod their head, as well, to avoid putting weight on the sore leg, but it could be the front or the back one. Listening and watching is an additional way to determine which leg is getting sore.

You feel with your hands to determine how clean their coat is and if you missed any places while grooming, especially under the belly, where you'd have to bend or crouch down to see clearly. You can feel if a horse's body temperature seems too high. He may not have been cooled properly after a workout or he could be running a fever.

Running a hand down a leg reveals which joint, tendon or ligaments have subtle inflammation. You can feel heat around the injured part, even if there is no swelling. A horse may not be actually lame, but may have a mild strain that shows up as heat in the area. It can be treated early before it becomes a bigger injury.

Most grooms consider horses as their friends. As a groom, you get to know each horse as an individual, their likes and dislikes, what they are afraid of and what relaxes them. There is a bond that forms when you work with them. Sometimes I'd wake in the night sensing something was wrong in the barn. I'd go out to check and find one of the horses might be sick or gotten cast - having rolled on their back and become stuck upside down with their legs against the wall. A horse's lungs are at the top of his ribcage, and if he lays too long on his back, the weight of his intestines and other organs begin to impair his breathing.

Horses communicate with each other in minute muscle twitches and tensions of body: neck, ears, back, the angle and turn of head. It is a silent language that speaks volumes. It shouts intent for those who learn to see and is a dance of undoing for those who don't read the signs right - half a ton of hurt and danger if you are unaware.

It is in these ways that grooms, riders and trainers talk to their horses, their bodies working off each other, responding and replying with the flick of an ear, the close of a hand. It is a ballet of communication and communion, a force that moves with that raw power of nature we are so fascinated with.

It is natural for horses to ride this crest of super-knowing. Humans train and direct this force for their own purposes. But that raw, coiled power of the instinct to survive is always there and can override even the best of training.

A local farm held a carriage event, a competition for horses pulling vehicles of all kinds. There were two-wheeled and four-wheeled carriages, covered and open, holding as few as one person or as many as five or six. Smaller carriages are pulled by a single horse or two horses side by side, called a pair. Two horses, one in front of the other, are called a tandem. The bigger carriages had four horses hitched together and are called four-in-hands. It was a pretty big event, with people bringing their horses from out of state to compete.

The horses and carriages were driven through the trails and fields on an obstacle course. I was enlisted to be an outrider. My job was to sit on horseback at a trail entrance into a stand of woods. Carriages went in, made a circle and came back out on the same path. I was there to make sure they emerged from the trees before the next carriage went in. Two teams of horses meeting face to face on a narrow trail with no room to turn around or pass each other would have been close to disastrous.

I was called back to the main staging area because there had been an accident. A carriage overturned at the starting point and the horses, breaking free from the carriage, bolted through the field past the spectators. Connected together by harness, the four horses careened down the drive and around a blind curve.

Coming up the drive were two young women who had recently obtained their drivers licenses. They saw a sign announcing the carriage event and thought they'd take a look.

Nothing stops instinctive tons running for their life. Not even a car. They ran right through it, breaking glass and ripping flesh, the calamity only urging onward the instinct to run. The two horses in front saw the car and tried to swerve. The ones behind didn't have a chance.

In the aftermath, I had been summoned to help pick up the pieces. Maroon pools of blood. Brass fittings snapped and twisted like soft putty. Ripped and shredded leather. The car was smashed, roof flattened – a total loss. The girls were miraculously unhurt, just a few cuts. They were taken to a nearby house and told to shower with their shoes on so their feet wouldn't be cut by the hundreds of shards of glass. The horses were taken to a veterinary center. They didn't all survive.

Horses pulse on strong waves of instinctive action, a flow of what nature gave them. This can save them or be their undoing, as well as the undoing of the people around them.

## Chapter 30

# Delaware Park

New horses continued to come to the farm while familiar ones left. After showing at Madison Square Garden in New York City, Roo Boo was purchased by his new owner. Moe left soon after Leegent. Moose was still at the farm and was ridden in fox hunts in the off-racing season by his owner. Horses that had finished their course of retraining were shipped back to their farms. Sneaky was trained to accept a saddle and rider, and continued his schooling.

Philbee wasn't raced in the deep part of winter. Lee took him to a small, indoor horse show and entered him in some jumping classes and a hack class – walk, trot and canter – where she rode him sidesaddle. He handled it all with the same equanimity he showed at the track and came home with a fourth-place ribbon. Later, in the spring, she raced him over fences at point-to-points. He was a versatile and athletic horse.

In the late fall, a local hunt club used the area for fox hunting. We sometimes joined in to give the horses that experience, too. Most of them were well-mannered, considering they'd been trained to run when around other horses.

We rode every day throughout the winter unless it was a blizzard out. We didn't have an indoor arena to ride in, so it was mostly the front field or trails. Basic groundwork and jumping went on, but it was no longer the main focus. With the infusion of new horses still in active racing careers, the attention shifted away from retraining. Now the horses were exercised with an eye for racing fitness.

At any given time, trainers have a choice of races at different tracks and try to select those competitions best suited for their horses. Lee trailered horses to run not only at Penn National near Hershey, Pennsylvania, but also at Keystone Racetrack – which became Philadelphia Park and is now Parx Casino and Racing. Some tracks, like Keystone and Penn National, ran all year round, while others had racing just in the warmer months of the year.

In late spring, Delaware Park, a track near the farm, opened for its annual summer season. With the track being so near – just half an hour away – we began taking horses there for morning exercise.

Built in the 1930s, Delaware Park was located in a peaceful setting of green hills. It was one of those old-time tracks where grass grows around the shed rows and large, leafy trees throw shade between the barns. The abundance of nature lent a sense of calm not often found on more modern tracks of cinder block and corrugated metal. In secluded corners under the trees, small cabins were home to grooms and assistant trainers. When the morning's work was done, you could see one or more of them sitting on the steps reading the Racing Form.

There is etiquette at racetracks, unwritten rules for exercising horses on the track and manners in the barn. Exercise gallops go counterclockwise - the direction races are run. Horses being given a workout at a full gallop have the right of way on the inside rail. Horses galloping at a moderate pace are kept to the center of the track, while those going slowest are ridden near the outside rail.

If you are out galloping and you hear a horse coming up fast behind you, you know they will pass on your left and you'd better not veer in or you will hear about it.

In the mornings, jockeys and exercise riders are not always silent on the backs of the horses. There is a lot of chirping, clicking, whistling and talking going on. Sometimes they encourage their mounts to go faster, "Get up, you! Pick up your feet," and sometimes they settle the horse, "Easy, easy now."

Riders sailed around the track in pairs or groups carrying on conversations. "Then the S.O.B. wanted to borrow my car, I told him..."

*World in a Shoe*

All this among the rhythmic bellows of the horse's breathing.

Occasionally, riders swore at each other, continuing some kind of a grudge. Some tried pick-up lines. Other times you were just admired. "Ooo-la-la, a pretty girl on a big horse," I once heard behind me. I looked over and a cute, dark-eyed jockey gave me a big grin as he passed at speed on my left.

Even during races, jockeys are not silent. If you ever have the opportunity to stand at the backside of the track, away from the grandstand as the horses run past, you'll hear the jockeys swearing and yelling. Over the thunder of the horses' hooves, there will be calls for more room and curses flung at each other – and sometimes at the horses, too. Sight, sound and colors blur by in seconds.

After the last horses returned from exercise, the frenzy of the early morning hours in the shed row calmed. The pace slowed. All that was left to do was cool down the horses and attend to the bits and pieces of finishing off the morning. Grooms whistled or talked quietly, going about their chores.

\* \* \* \*

I stopped for Lou Woodie to get a sip of water. Whether a race or morning exercise, the horses were always hot-walked afterward. He was just back from his morning gallop around the sandy oval. Philbee, Cosnav and Sneaky, already exercised, watched quietly from their stalls. I could feel the heat coming off Lou's body. We resumed walking, his mahogany head and black mane by my right shoulder.

To walk a horse around the shed row is to move through different environments of sight, sound and smell. Often, the barns are a mix of trainers – some with as few as one or two horses, others with up to ten or twenty, all housed under the same roof.

Each racing stable has their own colors, an identifying trademark of that particular trainer. Buckets, blankets, bandages, stall guards, even horse vans and trailers are painted in these hues. When a horse runs in a race, the jockey wears the colors of the horse's owner, which are usually different from the stable colors. If the trainer also happens to own the horse, then the jockey's colors are the same as those of the stable. Otherwise, each owner has their individual colors and designs. Lee had chosen cobalt blue and bright green for her colors.

A barn shared by many trainers presents a multitude of a sensory input. Along with the different stable colors, various fragrant, healing liniments and body washes are used on the horses. Even the grooms at each of the stables listen to their personal preference of music on dusty, beat-up radios often hanging from a nail.

In walking circuits around the barn, you might pass stalls displaying colors of yellow and black, the radio tuned to rock and roll, and smell Bigeloil in the horse's wash water. Go round the corner and you might come to a stable with dark green and white stall guards and feel the astringent bite of Absorbine liniment in your nose while classical music drifts in the air. Swing around to the back of the barn and find grooms doing their chores to disco music, the horses draped in yellow and purple coolers, and pass buckets of hot wash water laced with Vetrolin.

Grooms and hot walkers – people hired just for that job – made continuous circuits with horses throughout the morning. A set of rules kept order, and letting others know you were stopping was foremost among them. A loud, "Ho back!" alerted those behind you to pause at a distance so they wouldn't get kicked.

Most of our horses were good about being walked and followed your lead. Others wanted to walk you. A chestnut horse came to us for a short time. Hot walking him was like holding back a train with a strip of leather as it was leaving the station.

On turns around the barn, you might talk a bit in passing with the other grooms. Conversations carried on two or three sentences at a time throughout the morning – light talk, never giving out information about your horses. Though you shared the common bond of caring for horses, they were still the competition – if not in the next race, then perhaps one day down the road. If they asked, you told them "The horses were good." If someone seemed too keen to know, you put them off. The state of your horse's soundness and what was done to keep him that way was secret. Trainers made sure you knew that. If the trainer chose to share something with another trainer, that was their prerogative. As a groom, you never told "trade secrets."

\* \* \* \*

When the young bay filly stepped off the trailer the previous summer and surveyed her surroundings with an air of superiority, she promptly gained the nickname Viva.

Viva settled into her new routine and took to training with no complaints. She had perfect manners around the barn: stood when tied, wasn't ticklish being groomed and got along with the other horses. When it came time for Lee to get on her back for the first time, Viva hardly reacted. Within minutes, she was walking around like an old school horse.

With the basics of stop, steer and turn learned in the ring, it was time to take Viva out on some trails. She was a perfect angel. Not a spook or a shy out of her, and I wondered whether she would make any kind of a racehorse. The only thing she ever did was occasional short bucks, called crow hopping. Lee assured me Viva would perk up once she got to the track and her DNA kicked in.

It kicked in one summer morning at Delaware Park. Lee had taken some horses over for exercise and Susan, who was working for Lee on a summer program, rode Viva. It was Viva's first time on a racetrack. I was next to Susan and Viva on one of the older hoses to act as a stabilizing influence. Lee told us to trot once around the track, and then go around again at a slow hand gallop before heading back to the barn.

Lee rode Philbee that morning, wanting to give him a fast workout. Susan and I set off at a jog while Lee went ahead of us on Philbee. Viva was really well-behaved and quiet until the second pass down the homestretch.

Horses thundered by on our left. It was Lee on Philbee and I heard her yelling, "Hyah, Philbee! Get up! Get up!" Viva heard Lee, too, and took off. Susan quickly had her back under control. After that morning, Viva quit crow hopping and started running. She knew she was a racehorse.

At Viva's very first race, I was more nervous than I thought I'd be. I'd been part of this filly's daily routine since she'd come to the farm largely untrained. Now she was ready for her first start.

I was in the grandstand section down by the finish wire, near the gate where grooms collect their horses after a race. The murmuring, jostling crowd of spectators around me waited excitedly for the start.

The race was called a Maiden Race for horses who had not won their first race. Once a horse has "broken their maiden" – won their first race – they're not eligible to run in this kind of race anymore. Sometimes a horse wins the first time out, sometimes it takes two or three or more attempts before they cross the wire ahead of the others.

Viva had been quiet in the paddock for saddling, and having warmed up, she was now across the track with the other horses moving around at the starting gate. I couldn't make her out but knew she was there waiting her turn to be channeled into the narrow chute. Along with everything else, she'd had to learn to go in the gate and stand patiently. Horses that don't aren't allowed to run in races because it's too dangerous.

Although there are only seconds from the time the last horse is loaded to when the gate flies open, they are the longest and hardest seconds to bear. It seems there is a collective holding of breath where anticipation peaks and time stretches out.

For a moment, I remembered how Viva was to ride, her early crow-hopping and the day she took off at the track with Susan. I remembered the hundred other little things I'd gotten to know about this horse in the last year. All of Lee's training, long hours and hard work were for this moment.

Suddenly, the gate sprung open and the mass of heads and flying manes surged forward even before the sound of the bell reached the grandstand. The bunched, running field of horses elongated down the backstretch, the fastest ones taking the early lead.

It was all happening so quickly. Races are only minutes long, and yet can feel like forever. I kept seeing and losing sight of Viva through glimpses of her jockey's colors among the other vibrant hues. The horses shifted positions again going around the last turn, with new ones taking the lead while others dropped back as they tired.

They flew into the homestretch. The roar of the crowd grew to a crescendo. Voices around me speeding their favorites home, mine among them. I stood right at the wire. I wanted to see the moment she crossed the finish line.

She was not with the leaders, but in the middle of the pack trying her best. That was good enough for her first time out.

During hot walking, Viva was full of herself – prancing and shaking her head. She'd stop in alert stillness to listen as the crowd roared home another winner. After a minute, a little tremble went through her and she reluctantly resumed walking to cool down. Viva ran well for her first race.

She finally did break her maiden – win her first race - though I wasn't there to see it. She ran well on dirt, but excelled on turf, which is a grass course.

Turf is more commonly found on European tracks, while the most common surface in the United States is dirt. Many racetracks in the U.S. also have a turf course within the larger dirt oval. However, turf courses are used infrequently in comparison to dirt tracks, which are used virtually every day.

Some horses prefer turf and run their best races on it. I don't know if it had anything to do with her early training and trail rides at the farm, but Viva came into her own when she was on grass.

*World in a Shoe*

## Chapter 31

# Just Business

A racing-fit Thoroughbred is like an entirely different species of animal. They look like other horses, but have a finely tuned nervous system and quick reflexes. Fed high-powered diets and exercised to a fine pitch, they become tight as a spring. Through exercising, that spring is wound tighter and tighter until the energy is ready to be released in a race. Once expended, the process of exercising, feeding and building the energy starts again. Over and over, it is the cycle for racehorses.

Some trainers give their horses time off. They send them to the farm for a change of pace and scenery. This helps their mind and overall health. But more often than not, especially with the cheaper class of horses, they may spend years of their lives at the track.

In the days I worked there, some trainers tried to get away with illegally drugging their horses. Trainers often used pain medication to help a horse recover from an injury. But there were unethical ones who found ways to circumvent drug testing to run an injured horse on painkillers instead of letting it rest and recover. They continued to run it to make money. Sometimes they would administer steroids, and even hormones such as testosterone, which made the horses more aggressive. This led to some mean-tempered and even paranoid animals.

The horses had little quirky ways to deal with the stress. If they lashed out or tried to bite in a fit of temper, it was to be overlooked. The horses always came first – they were the ones earning the paycheck. I heard tell of grooms suffering broken bones, getting kicked or bitten. They were not allowed to discipline the horses. If they did, they lost their jobs. More than once at the track I heard, "Grooms and hot walkers are expendable. They are a dime-a-dozen. But good racehorses cannot be replaced."

Some horses were real maniacs to try and deal with: rearing, spinning, and dragging you as though you were a paper doll. "Never let the horses go," they tell you. "At all costs hang on, they are worth more than your life." So you hung on.

One story I heard at the track stayed with me: "A horse got loose from its groom. Cranked in high gear, it ran blindly and fast into the solid, broad side of the barn as though it were air."

Our horses were lucky in that Lee believed in giving them time off where they could amble in a pasture and relax in nature. She even gave them supplements from the health food store. She never resorted to drugging the horses, and if they were ever sore enough to need pain medication, they were given time off to heal. Our horses were all pretty sane, although somewhat eager and determined to take you for exercise instead of vice versa.

The cycle of horses arriving at and leaving the farm continued. Philbee went to his new home with a woman who planned to use him as a show horse. A little chestnut horse named Johnny left, so did Siren and Carly, who had gotten over her fear of crossing streams. A gentle gray mare named Mockingbird was sent to her new owner. Impulsive Decision, a bay mare we nicknamed D.C., arrived to become part of the racing stable.

I purchased Honky Tonk, a buckskin mare – not a Thoroughbred – that I'd known from a previous job at another farm. She was great fun, and I showed her and rode the trails.

I don't know if it was her tan coloring, but deer didn't bound away when we rode by. One day while riding Honky Tonk, we walked out of a tree line and entered a field. We were surrounded by white-tailed deer walking with us – some of them close enough I could've reached out and touched them.

I played a game with her I called tiger in the grass. I'd creep out low to the ground when she was in the pasture. She knew it was me, but went along with it. Head up, ears pricked forward, she'd give long, blowing snorts and cavort with her tail over her back. I'd creep some more, she'd rear, buck and kick, running in circles around me. As soon as I stood, her whole body relaxed and she'd put her head down, ambling over to be petted.

In the fall, Delaware Park closed and Lee rented stabling at Garden State Park in New Jersey. The grandstand at Garden State Park had burned down a couple of years before, and although there was no racing, the facility was open for training horses. Lee got an allotment of stalls and a room for hay, feed and storing equipment. We shipped some of the horses to stay at Garden State Park and every day made the one-hour commute each way to care for them. It was a sparse place with wooden barns, graveled walkways and asphalt.

Having horses stabled in two places made the workdays longer. Our daily routine started on the farm by feeding and turning out the horses, then driving to the track to arrive by 6 a.m. to feed those horses.

While the horses ate, I refilled the hay nets with alfalfa and set them aside. I'd check the exercise schedule, arrange the tack for each horse and get the first one prepared to go out. The racetrack itself was only open until 10 in the morning. We had to work quickly so the horses had time to get their exercise.

Lee rode them herself or hired exercise riders while I did the work on the ground. In the space of twenty-five minutes or so, while the horse was out for exercise, I cleaned the stall, bedded it with fresh straw, scrubbed the feed tub and water bucket, then brushed and got the next horse ready to go. I worked at a lively pace.

Once the horses came back from the track, they were washed and walked cool. Their legs were felt for heat or swelling, and poultices, liniments and bandages were applied as needed. Final grooming was done, tack cleaned, aisle raked, tools put away and the horses given their noontime meal.

At that point, we'd head back to the farm, grab lunch and follow a similar routine with the horses there. We could be a little more relaxed on the farm. There wasn't the pressure of time unless one of the horses was running in a race that night. I rode more of the farm horses, continuing with basic retraining. We often weren't finished with the day until well after dark.

We made the hour drive to the track and back every day – even during blizzards. When the weather was really bad and the horses were only going to be walked round the shed row, I'd make the trip by myself. I left extra early if it was snowing. Even with snow tires, my little green Datsun didn't have a lot of traction. I'd put one of Lee's anvils in the back seat for extra weight and maneuver in behind the row of state-run snowplows going down the freeways at 5 in the morning.

No matter the weather, one or both of us was at the track each day. Sometimes when we got busy, Lee hired Bill to hot walk for us. Bill was retired and had always loved racing. With so much free time on his hands, he applied to walk "hots" at the track. He'd check in with different stables in the morning to see who needed a hand. Calm and patient, he got to know all our horses and they seemed to like him.

He read the Daily Racing Form avidly to see which horses were running. As far as I know, he never placed an actual money bet on a race, but did what he called paper bets. He said he was pretty good at it.

Having horses stabled at the track and spending half the day there was to become part of the fabric of track life. It was exposure to the side of racing that was more business. For some people, horses were just a commodity. Some outrageous, exotic and painful things occurred at the track.

There were many exercise riders available for hire. Some of them were jockeys who rode races later in the day. Others couldn't make it as jockeys and became exercise riders. I remember one rider some trainers used. He was old, alcoholic and showed up drunk for work each morning. One of the times I saw him, he was laying on the horse's neck, just about falling off. He never fell, there weren't any accidents, and the horses never ran away with him. I think they must have taken care of him.

One trainer had a pet cougar. Dogs weren't supposed to be in the stable area, as they might chase the horses. Cats were good for catching mice and rats, so technically, they were allowed. Whether he used this rationale or not I don't know, but in any event, he regularly brought his pet cougar to the track with him. I had heard about the cougar and was curious. This trainer was stabled at one of the tracks where we occasionally raced our horses, so I'd have to wait to catch a glimpse of it when we were there.

One day I did see it. I was walking one of our horses back to the visitor's barn from a race when I saw the big tawny cat laying in a fenced pen. I wanted to see more, go back and look closer, but I had a horse to cool down.

We heard about an instance where someone snuck into a horse's stall the night before it was to race and hit it in the leg with a hammer. It wasn't enough to break bone, but the groom found him in the morning lame as could be. There was a big bet going – if the horse had run and beat the competition, the people would have lost everything.

The culprit was eventually found. He had been paid to hit that horse.

I experienced a situation like this first-hand when D.C. ran and won a race. On and off she'd had some soreness in her knees. If there was ever any question on her soundness, she wasn't run.

D.C. was fine for this particular race where she ran wire to wire – first out of the gate, first across the finish. The owners of the second-place horse were screaming and yelling threats at us. They'd been led to believe D.C. wasn't sound enough to win and had mortgaged their house and placed everything on their horse crossing the line first.

Other people's treatment of their horses filtered back to us. Grooms, pony riders and others passed on news and gossip.

"That trainer with the horse that ran twenty times and it didn't bring home a check? He collected the insurance on it."

*I don't get it, what do they mean?* I felt naive, standing there with a question on my face.

"They stood him in the whirlpool bath and left the electric cord hanging near him – he liked to chew, that horse." Horses will sometimes chew things when they are bored, standing around.

"They can get a better horse now with the insurance money – one that will win them a check for once."

There were other stories about crooked vets that put horses with minor injuries down, and then provided an accident report and death certificate so insurance could be collected. Money passed hands – it was just business.

*Chapter 32*

# Any Vet to the Track

"Any vet to the track, there's a horse down."

The announcement came over the loudspeakers at the barn. My heart sank a little whenever I heard a call for a veterinarian. I didn't like to think of any horse sick or injured.

The vets made daily rounds among the stables, but sometimes there were emergencies in the barn or on the track and you'd hear a call over the loudspeakers.

"Any vet to the track." Again the announcement.

Lee and I had come in to Garden State at the break of dawn to exercise and care for the horses. Because the oval track closed each morning at 10, we worked quickly and with efficient focus to get the horses out. I'd boosted Lee up onto Cosnav's back close to twenty minutes ago, about how long the horses were normally out for exercise.

Most of the work for the other horses was done, and they were chewing their hay contentedly. All that was left of the late morning's chores was grooming, bandaging, cleaning tack and the noon feed.

Lee and Cosnav were due back any minute. He was the last to go out and I'd already cleaned his stall, scrubbed his water and feed buckets, and gotten hay ready for him.

Holding a half-rolled flannel bandage, I stepped out of the tack room, listening to the third call for a vet. I looked right and didn't see them. I looked left and saw the other horses watching me, their focus entirely on me.

Perhaps it was the way they were all looking at me. Viva, Lou, Nahma, D.C. They knew, and in that instant I knew, too. It was Cosnav.

I so deeply didn't want it to be him that I shoved the knowing aside. Instead, I headed in the direction of the track to meet Lee on her way back.

My mind ran with thoughts. *She'll be along in a minute - she's on the path, just behind that barn, I'll see her in a second.*

It was eerie. Other grooms were walking out toward the track, too. Like me, they expected their charges back at any moment. There was a group of us moving together, not meeting each other's eyes but searching among the approaching riders and horses, each seeking a familiar face, hoping for the feeling of relief. I caught snippets of conversations among the other grooms.

"Do you know who it is?"

"A blue and green cap."

"Don't know who."

"A brown horse."

As the riders reached our group, grooms turned to walk back to the stables with their horses.

I was the only one left.

An ambulance pulled away as I reached the entry chute to the track. One of the track attendants said the rider was talking and seemed okay but they were taking them to the hospital to get checked.

The familiar dark blue station wagon of our vet, Richard, drove up. He was working at the track that morning and happened to respond to the call.

"I think it's Lee on Cosnav." I said.

"Hop in, let's go see."

I rode out with Richard to the area of the track just past the turn. Beneath the rails, I could see a dark form on the ground. My heart seemed to stop.

It was Cosnav, my friend. How did this happen? How could he have fallen?

He was trying to get up, pushing with his front legs while the back ones were scrabbling. He was unable to get them under himself. Gawkers stood around staring.

"Hit the rail, flipped over it," someone said.

I could only see little Cosnav, so afraid of small things and yet brave against big things. Bill walked out to us. It was a comfort, he knew Cosnav, too.

It was hard to determine how badly he was injured. Being unable to use his legs could mean a broken bone or nerve damage in the spine.

"Maybe he's just stunned," Richard said.

He listened to Cosnav's heart and lungs, said they sounded clear and strong. If he'd broken his back and there was nerve damage, then most likely there would be problems with his heart and breathing.

"Sometimes they can be temporarily stunned. Let's roll him over, maybe he can get up from his other side," he suggested. We did, and tried to push Cosnav's legs under him, but still he could only use his front legs.

A tractor and trailer with a winch had pulled up. "That horse dead yet?" came a voice from a walkie-talkie. "Hurry up, we want to go home."

Once more we turned Cosnav over. His eye was covered in sand and he was unable to blink – signs of nerve damage. He struggled less and less, losing his beautiful, sleek body bit by bit. I could see he was going.

"Richard, you'd better put him down."

The injection.

Richard listened.

No heartbeat.

I never knew how cooperative a horse was until I had to lift Cosnav's head when he was dead. He was so heavy I could barely get the bridle off. Bill had to help me.

Richard drove us back to the barns while the trailer and tractor moved in to remove Cosnav from the track. To them, he was no more than trash – just something in the way of someone going home.

I needed to call Neil and go to the hospital to check on Lee. Richard said he was going to do an autopsy on Cosnav to see what had happened. Cosnav's body would lay temporarily behind a building near the front gate, and sometime during the day a truck from a rendering plant would pick him up. I didn't look forward to the autopsy, but out of a sense of duty, I felt I had to go. I told Richard I'd find him after I got back. When I called, Neil said he was going straight to the hospital.

At the hospital, the doctors said Lee had a concussion. She was lucky. She could go home but could not go back to work or ride for a month – and to not upset her. I was wondering how I was going to do that with what had happened to Cosnav. But she figured it out.

"Where's Cosnav?" Lee asked from the bed when she saw me.

"He's at the track." I replied, entering the room.

"How is he?"

"He's fine now."

"Is he in his stall?"

"No."

"He's dead, isn't he?"

I could only shake my head.

She showed me the Caliente helmet she had been wearing. It had a big crease down the side where her head had hit the racetrack railing when she fell. She'd have been dead, too, if it weren't for that helmet.

I told her Neil was coming and I would take care of the horses at the track before heading back to the farm. Neil picked up Lee at the hospital and went home. They didn't come by the track.

\* \* \* \*

The ocean.

That's what Cosnav's body smelled like all opened up. I was surprised. I hadn't known what to expect – anything but the ocean. The salt, clean smell made it somehow all right to walk around the loose coils of intestines.

Richard had checked his heart and lungs, which were fine. He then showed me the long incision in Cosnav's neck and pulled back the flesh to reveal the vertebrae that had been fractured.

"His neck was broken in two places," Richard said. "He should have died almost instantly. I don't know why he lived as long as he did."

*My little friend, you had heart right up to the end.*

Back at the barn, Cosnav's empty stall felt like too much. I raked back the bedding and cleaned the saddle and bridle, taking the bit off to thoroughly wash away the blood. Bill had gone back ahead of me to feed and water the other horses.

I was alone finishing up. The groom from down the shed row, the one with a favorite chestnut-colored horse with white socks, came and stood for a time, watching me.

"You have to go on," he said. "It's hard to lose them, but you have to go on with life." He stayed and talked to me for a time.

If I could share with him now, I'd tell him, "*You came and it felt like you were the only one to say anything that really touched me. From others I heard 'Tough break,' and 'Well, at least he wasn't an expensive one.' But you knew. You were one of the ones who knew the greater connection – the breathing in your soul that horses are. Thank you.*"

At the time, I blamed myself for Cosnav's accident. Although it turned out to be the failure of a new piece of equipment that I barely saw before he went out for his workout, I still felt I'd failed to keep him safe.

I was so busy I didn't have time to process what had happened. There was so much work, and I was doing it by myself while Lee recuperated. She ran the business from the house. I drove to the track every day to care for and oversee the horses, then drove back to the farm to clean stalls and ride the horses there.

It seemed I felt Cosnav's loss more than many of the people around me. They commented "too bad" and got on with life. I tried to do the same, but it didn't work. To me, it was more than losing a horse. It was losing a friend who, though an animal, had every bit of individual personality as any human being.

We later heard that someone went out to Cosnav's body before it was removed from the track grounds and cut off his penis. They left it in a tack box to be found the next morning – some kind of payback or revenge.

At the track, I fed the horses and got them ready for exercise. Hired riders took them out. I did everything the same, mucking stalls and grooming the horses. But nothing felt the same. There was a hollowness inside.

I didn't know it, but my life was changing direction away from horses. Like a ship changing course, the shift was imperceptible at first. It wasn't a change I would have willingly embraced. Horses were my life.

There were little signs of the coming change. One morning, hot walking Nahma around the shed row, I stopped for him to get a sip of water. He lifted his head and looked at me – looked right through me. Something reached out and touched me, a force much greater than Nahma or me, greater than life and death itself. It was only a moment, and while I'd like to say that my pain was gone, it wasn't. But, it was reduced. Something in me had made a bit of peace somewhere.

It was a time of loss leading to change. My envisioned future was shifting out from under me. Not just Cosnav, but another loss was about to impact my life.

*Chapter 33*

# Rodeo Cowboy

    Shortly before Cosnav's accident, I took a vacation to see my mom. She lived out in the desert in California. One morning, I took a trail ride at the local stable that offered guided rides into the desert. Our leader was a handsome young man named Sam who took an interest in me.
    I went to the stables again for more trail rides. Sam and I hit it off and began seeing each other every day while I was there. He liked horses as much as I did. He told me he was a rodeo cowboy and was doing work at the ranch in the off-season. During the summers, he traveled the rodeo circuit riding bareback competitions. We spent many hours talking about our horse worlds. I didn't know much about rodeo and he was interested in the world of the track. Though I had dated other guys, I felt most like myself with Sam.
    We did other things besides riding. On one of my last evenings there, we took a tram 8,516 feet above the walls of Chino Canyon to a restaurant at the top, where we had dinner.
    There, Sam told me, "I could spend a long, long time with you."
    I felt I could spend a long time with him as well.
    He asked me if I'd ever been camping on horseback. I hadn't. He had family in Colorado and suggested we meet up there, pack our gear and head into the wilderness on horseback to camp for a bit. Even though I'd only known this guy for a couple of weeks, in that moment I thought, *Why not try it?*

I decided I'd give notice to Lee on returning from vacation. I told Sam I'd need some time before leaving my position at Lee's so they could find and train a replacement.

I headed back to Pennsylvania and the farm excited about this new life adventure. Lee received the news pretty well, but was a bit disappointed to lose me, I think. She and Neil made some jokes about me "being in love" and not being into my work as much. I stayed in touch with Sam through letters and phone.

Then Cosnav's accident happened. There was so much to do, and with Lee injured, leaving as soon as I'd planned was out of the question. I phoned Sam and told him I needed to delay leaving by at least a month. He said he was okay with it.

Lee got better and things began to return to normal at the barn. I was finally in a place where I could think about leaving. Lee hired and trained a couple of girls to take over the work at the barn and track.

Sam and I stayed in touch. We still planned to meet in Colorado. I was going to fly out once he got there. He told me he was ready to leave his job at the ranch.

"I'm driving from here to Colorado," he said. "It'll take me about three days. I'll call you when I get in."

That was the last I ever heard from him.

I waited the three days. When I didn't hear from him, I waited another couple of days, then called the ranch. I thought perhaps he had delayed leaving or decided not to go.

"He's not here. We thought he was with you," they told me.

I waited a few more days and checked in again. No, they hadn't heard from him. I didn't have any contact information for his family in Colorado, though somehow I got the impression from talking to people at the ranch that his family hadn't heard from him, either. Nor were his friends at the ranch too concerned he hadn't turned up. He was a transient kind of guy and would show in his own time.

I had no way to contact him and didn't know what had happened. Did he change his mind, deciding he liked his freedom more than me? Or had he been in some kind of accident? I tried to explain it to myself.

Grieving Cosnav's loss and blaming the incident on myself, it wasn't too far a jump to feel I deserved Sam's abandonment.

Years later, while doing emotional-clearing work around these incidents, I found that I was – on a deep level – relieved Sam hadn't called. With maturity and hindsight, I remember him drinking a lot and often being drunk. I discovered I was actually a little bit afraid of him. It was probably for the best we didn't reconnect.

At the time, I felt I had to go anyway; to make my own journey without him. I no longer had the job with Lee, and I needed to get away and sort things out for myself.

I packed a bag, sold my car and flew to the West Coast. There, I bought a used car. I drove aimlessly, following roads that looked inviting and traveled to towns with interesting names. I slept in the car. I read spiritual literature. I picked up hitchhikers. I was looking for answers to what was happening inside me.

After weeks of driving, I felt it was time to return to Pennsylvania. I drove back across the country and returned to the farm. I had maintained the rent on my apartment, so I had a place to stay. I had no answers that I could voice, but the inner changes continued.

Less and less did I feel the connection to horses I once had. It was confusing. I'd never lost a part of me before and didn't know the signs of a way of life coming to an end. I was unhappy within myself. My internal ground was shifting so much. I was out of balance and needed to find some stability.

*World in a Shoe*

*World in a Shoe*

## Chapter 34

# My Door's Always Open to You

The shift away from horses didn't happen all at once, but it had begun. My life was changing, going in another direction. The message just hadn't caught up with me yet. I was at loose ends. I hadn't found the healing answers I'd been seeking. I sought stability, but didn't know what form that stability might take.

I still had my apartment at the farm and took walks in the fields. Every other day or so, I walked to the barn. One of the boarders asked me to recommend someone to float her horse's teeth. I knew of horse dentists in the area, but for some reason Mr. Heffner came to mind. I don't know why, but I gave her his name and number.

I didn't know if he'd even drive that far to work on her horse. I wasn't sure I wanted to see him – I'd walked away four years before and hadn't said a word to him since. I didn't know if he'd want to see me, either.

One afternoon, I went down to the barn and saw his old, bronze-colored car in the driveway. I hesitated, undecided whether to stay or go back. I decided to brave it and walked toward the barn. I told myself the worst that could happen was he wouldn't say anything to me, just finish up his work and go.

Before I reached the barn, he came out carrying his halter, ropes, stainless-steel bucket and short stool.

He saw me. Without pause, he spoke.

"How you doing, Kid?"

He was walking to his car. "Come and talk to me."

It was as if there had been no break between us. Perhaps he saw I was hurting and in need of help. I don't remember the details of the conversation, but one thing has stayed with me.

He said, "My door's always open to you, Kid."

I knew I'd hurt him when I walked away. Yet no matter what, he'd taken me back.

He told me to come for dinner. I began going to his house regularly, only this time we talked about spiritual things. We did talk about horses a bit, too, and he helped me with healing one of the horses at the farm. Beyond the application of the remedies, he spoke to me about how to use prayer and energy to augment the healing.

For a time, I persisted in thinking I could get back to horses and the connection I'd once had. One of the final things Mr. Heffner taught me, though it came in the form of a riding lesson, was something valuable about myself.

I was riding his wife's horse, Obi. Mr. Heffner had me jumping the same fence in the ring. Each time, he put the fence a little higher. At one point I cantered Obi up to it, but he put on the brakes, stopping at the last minute, and I went over the fence without him.

Mr. Heffner got me back on the horse and explained my fear of jumping the fence was what caused Obi to refuse. "He felt you hesitating and he stopped."

When I looked at it, I saw he was right. Every time he raised the fence, I got a little more nervous. I hadn't seen that in myself. I understood Obi was uncertain about jumping the fence because of my feelings.

Mr. Heffner continued. "Kid, don't ever let anyone try to convince you to do something you're afraid to do – that's how people get hurt."

It takes a certain kind of fearlessness to jump a cross-country course of four- and five foot-high fences or navigate a timed round of high show-jumping fences. Not all riders have it in their nature to compete at that level.

"There's no shame in being timid of jumping over a certain height," he told me. "There's plenty you can do with a horse without jumping fences."

I need to say that not every fall from a horse is caused by fear. There are many valid reasons for accidents to occur. What he was getting at were instances where people put themselves in situations because they want to prove something. It could be potentially dangerous.

It was a valuable lesson to learn. While it took some time, I accepted it about myself.

I thought back and realized I had put myself in situations with horses I'd have been better off staying away from in the first place. Thanks to the graciousness and training of the horses I was on, I rarely got hurt.

Though the life of horses had let go of me, I hadn't yet let go of it. I struggled against the inevitable change that was coming. Mr. Heffner helped me a lot during this time, and I spent many evenings at his table, sharing meals with him and his family.

More and more our discussions were about spiritual things. It didn't surprise me at the time, but he pulled out articles and books about different spiritual teachers, mainstream and otherwise. Some I followed up on. These paved a new direction for me.

*World in a Shoe*

*Chapter 35*

# World in a Shoe

It was a slow process for me to let go of the life that had been my focus and felt so familiar, but exploring new spiritual directions felt right. It was time for me to take a step toward that new life.

I left the farm with all of its healing places. Working for Lee was a job I loved. Often at one with the horses, I felt every inch of who I was meant to be. The commune was total. Then it was gone.

I was never as confident. The ephemeral believing in myself had disappeared. Something had gone. I missed it; yet, at the same time, I didn't.

A few months later, I left the horse world entirely. I needed to cut myself loose from who I was and go on a search for who I was becoming. A journey of discovery awaited.

\* \* \* \*

For years, I had in my keeping a five-inch world in a horse's shoe. This time it was Cosnav's shoe.

At the autopsy, I had asked the vet to pull one of his racing plates. I didn't know why, but I felt I wanted it.

From time to time, I held it in my hand, perhaps hoping to divine something out of its depths to explain the loss. More than just Cosnav, a complete way of life went with him. Though it never contained a photo, it circled the memories in my heart of all my time with horses.

They are great creatures, spiritual beings and a path of honor and integrity for those willing to be embraced by it. Horses won't let you be otherwise. They make you reach for the best in yourself.

# Epilogue

Shortly after I finished working for Lee, the government got involved in investigating the drug abuse and treatment of horses at racetracks. Things have improved over the years through stricter monitoring and laws.

The events at the Devon Horse Show were totally my experience. In no way do I blame or hold responsible the Devon Horse Show Foundation, directors or administrators for the events that I write about.

While I write about some unusual and different techniques I experienced in working with horses, I was under the guidance of professionals at the time I learned about them. I encourage you to seek competent trainers in your area to help you with your horses.

I had a lot of free rein as a child. My mother drank and much of the time I didn't have adult guidance. I was able to finally heal and forgive my upbringing and my mother. This is the subject of my first book, "Doors to Transformation: My Mother My Self," available on Amazon.

*World in a Shoe*

# Acknowledgments

I am eternally grateful to my writing coach and publishers, Bonnie Groessl and Mike Dauplaise, for your gracious patience in my process with this book.

Mahalo, Mary Ke, for your perceptual eye to what worked and didn't work in the manuscript.

Thank you, Bev, for proofreading.

Thank you, Linda, for your reading and input, for being my "home away from home" and an ear for me to vent.

Thank you, Vima, for your loving support through all my challenges.

Thank you to everyone who was a voice of encouragement along the way. Your support added fuel for me to continue the manuscript to completion.

*Carrie Mackey Photography*

# About the Author

Nicole Lawrence is an eclectic soul who has followed her heart to experience careers featuring horses, visionary painting, fine art, event promotion, and exploration of many spiritual modalities. Metaphysics, the New Age, alternative health and healing trends have fascinated her for years.

Never one to follow trends, Nicole's life is a complex mix of ideas and values. She appreciates the stability and familiarity of convention, while at the same time is drawn to the "edge of newness," that edge beyond the boundary which gives birth to innovation.

Nicole views life as running in cycles and spirals, comprising the healing journeys we undertake as a regular part of our lives. Although no longer involved with horses, she feels this part of her life had a lasting and profound impact, an impact that influenced other areas in her life in terms of integrity, commitment and attention to detail.

www.ingramcontent.com/pod-product-compliance
Lightning Source LLC
LaVergne TN
LVHW052100090426
835512LV00036B/2857